Teenager or Adult

Teenager or Adult

✦

Do we deserve to drink alcohol?

Andrew Cornell

iUniverse, Inc.
New York Lincoln Shanghai

Teenager or Adult
Do we deserve to drink alcohol?

iUniverse books may be ordered through booksellers or by contacting:

iUniverse
2021 Pine Lake Road, Suite 100
Lincoln, NE 68512
www.iuniverse.com
1-800-Authors (1-800-288-4677)

ISBN: 0-595-34947-1

Printed in the United States of America

Contents

Interlude

I have created a book that is going to allow parents and future teenagers to the upper levels a "heads up" on alcohol. I am not an expert, but I have put in thousands of hours of research to complete my book. Many books are written that are a little bit similar to this one, but are not considered direct information to me. Most books in this category are written from a parent that has lost a child from alcohol. I am a teenager telling of certain issues involved with alcohol that debate controversy to what should be done. Some say that drinking should be illegal, that you should be twenty five to drink, and that teenagers should be able to drink. All of these issues are included on how you can deal with alcohol in the future. Also, included in this book are personal stories that I find a lot of humor in and many issues that teenagers will face as I complete my last year as a teenager. I speak as a teenager and this is the difference with my book being unique. I offer new ways to deal with alcohol that have not even been considered yet, that I believe will work much better. My point with this book is to save lives and stop premature death with people. I analyze the true reasons for why kids drink and drive and why they drink at all. I bring new ways for kids to drink safely, responsibly, and on terms that will not damage the body like it is said, but allow for parties to continue and the drinking to also staying on track. The only reason that I have decided to write something that is different from every other book on this same subject is that nothing is working. There needs to be a major change or the problem is going to get worse. In a world where problems get more diverse and we become smarter on objecting can only allow for the cross cancellation to stopping teenage drinking. As society accepts drinking more and more and allows for alcohol to become present in our lives increases everyday can only feed the fire, by helping my argument. There is nothing that can be done to stop a teenager from drinking completely so I have developed new ways of management to save more lives than we do today. My main purpose may seem cruel to some people, but all I would like to do is provide a few new procedures in hope that I can save lives.

I always like to start off with a funny story or something that people can relate to in a very early stage of my project. This will allow my readers to understand what I am going to blabber about for the majority of this book. Well, I am going to make that a second paragraph portion. My name is Andrew Cornell and I am not going to edit anything in this book besides grammar and punctuation. This means that the language, theme, and all stories are going to relate from a teenager's viewpoint. You will hear it like your kids say behind your back. Some of the other reasons for the lack of editing are that I bought a motorcycle and could not afford to have the book edited professionally. For all you crazy ass parents that find this book in your child's room, then just leave it there. This book does talk about teenage drinking, but it does it in a way to prevent the dangerous actions taken while drinking and mainly at parties. (They will go to them whether you want them to or not, but I will tell you how to work with them on it). Some of the things that are talked about support both sides of drinking. That means that I am not out to try and legalize the substance, but to explain some of the wrongful accusations towards teenagers. Both sides of the issues are covered and this includes teenagers drinking and teenagers not drinking. I will not go into so much detail that you are offended. Although I would love to do this, because its fun for a teenager, but that will be a second book titled "I Hope Your Offended". I do use the same language in this book that I would use at any party or other event that I would attend. Many teenagers use awful language, but mine is within reason and to grab your attention to know where I would like for you to pay extra attention. I am creating this book since it has been on my mind for a while and I will have it much harder to write then you will to read, and some things I believe are not spotlighted to the public well enough, plus my family will probably disown me for the controversies that I am accepting with writing this book. (Yes that was a run on sentence and I like them a lot since I can cram more between periods and run on sentences kick ass)(About the controversies though, bring them on because I know it will help sell my book and I really don't care, but I do care about making teenage life more efficient and safer). I know all the rules of grammar and sentence structure, and scored off the charts on the English part of the A.C.T. assessment test, but I am telling you to shut the hell up about that because its much more enjoying for me to write my book, this way, because it will allow you to go to this place in your mind that I am talking about if you can read it with the authors standing and true tone in mind (another run on, get my point). This means that different writing styles will be switched back and forth allowing for more variation for my chosen words. I am currently 18 years old and I believe that I have experienced some great stories and talk about some things that people should work out in certain ways or I hope to inspire you to have ideas on working out your problems. By the time that this book is published I will be almost twenty. Of course I have only seen a small portion compared to some readers, but I have recorded many good notes on these subjects through observations. Well I promised you a story pretty early in the book so here it goes. Actually I want to say a few more things first. This book talks about normal teenage problems and issues that the majority is subject to. I am not just going to talk about things like when I got too drunk and sprayed cars with a fire extinguisher or stories of people pissing on the R.A's door to their dorm. The point of this book is to attack the reasons for these things and much more. I want to speak of why kids drink and drive, and why they choose to drink no matter what the consequences are. The difference between my book and other teenage drinking books is that the point of view is from someone who has done all of the things that the controversy stands for and I can entertain you better than a sleazy statistician reading numbers. All of the other books that I have read on this subject are from people who grew up a long time ago and think that trying to stop the drinking is the only way. I do not think that this is the best method, but if that is what you are set on, than there are a few suggestions later on for doing this. This book tells of how the teenage drinking can either be made more efficient or how it can be fixed if needed. Here is the story that I promised you (I hope you like it.)

I have many friends that I love and we trust each other like a family. We all have nicknames and ours usually involve things that relate to something that happened in the past. For example EDC Dirty HP or G-Spence (This is due to lots of girls or guys and I will explain later along with my own nickname.) One time me and a couple of friends by the names of Dompa, Owen, Gandy (me), price master (I think, cant remember exactly who was there) and some other people were hanging out at a dead end to a street which was one of the best times of my life. When you have a certain place that you go to and you get a warm feeling about being there, but then you hate to leave because its so peaceful then try not to let it go (you will miss it). All teenagers have a place that they hang out at, which eventually will be gone and no other place you move onto for the rest of your life will ever be the same. This house involves complete seclusion from the big city with a big pool house, great pool and basically a great setting for a secluded teenage hangout spot. This was nice living for my friend who used to live there. Many great stories come from this amazing house that we cherished and anything that we broke was an accident and we always felt very sad for this and offered to pay for it. Well anyways the story goes that we would sit at the end of this road enjoying the weekends and yes we did a lot of drinking and other things, but what the hell, you get one shot at life and I will be damned if I am not going to enjoy every last minute of it. This one night we were sitting out there and finished off most of a half gallon of ___ hill vodka (not putting brand names cause I don't want to get sued for linking their company to underage drinking) and a Thirty P (Thirty Pack) of beer before 10 o'clock at night. We were still waiting for more people to show up and well a car came down the road that was a similar model and color as one we were expecting that I thought was one of our friends (it was nighttime and there was no streetlight). So we all decided to stumble over near the woods on the side of the road and we were going to attack our friend that was coming out to visit and scare the shit out of him. Well the car got to the gate and stopped because we shut it so they would get out and open it. We ran towards the car and started beating and crawling on top from out of nowhere. We heard a female scream inside so we figured that the more people with him, the more we would get to scare. We opened the doors to grab the people and being drunk like we were kind of exceeded the fact that we did not even know exactly who we were grabbing at. Well, when the dome light to the car finally turned on we saw a bunch of old people who looked like they just got out of church and got lost in the woods. These old people spun around and drove off like retired race car drivers and we just kind of stood there for a few minutes speechless of the whole thing looking at each other. I was personally stunned of what we just did to some random people. Then we all simultaneously started laughing our asses off about the whole idea because I know that I would have been scared if someone did that to me. Since we were lucky no one got killed or had a heart attack then we just simply went back to drinking and having a good time. The look on these peoples face was the most scared I think they have ever been and I would definitely have apologized but I think that's the last time they will get lost in the woods again. See teenagers are capable of teaching elders some things and even if they almost kill them in the process.

Okay enough of that, I am going to stop talking about the story that I regret pretty badly and talk about the theme of what I am writing about. I am not going to just talk about drunk incidents like people falling and putting their heads through walls or my best friends pissing on each others snow covered cars since I think there is just a little bit more to life. I am also not just saying that teenagers only piss and break stuff when they drink. Other issues will be about how young people can screw up parties by letting officers end them early when I have researched some cool loopholes that I have experienced and saved jail time and still kept the party going. To all parents though, I would like to explain later in this book that the loop holes are for your child's safety and not to walk all over police, but to bring back what has been lost from a teenager's lifestyle. This is the life of partying in a teenager's hard earned extra spare time. Teenagers take on as much responsibility through working, household responsibilities and classes at advanced levels to allow comparisons to an adult and more. Teenagers deserve to party as much as any adult and there is no stopping it, but there is ways to avoid the troublesome parts associated with it. Why the hell should teenagers be viewed as the ones who party, but the police and parents act surprised when they find the ones who do it? There are certain types of parties that I would like to talk about and mainly what types of college parties there are through thousands of miles of traveling to them (that is how I do research, lol). Plus there are certain ways to save you of being embarrassed in front of **hatchas** (kinda nice or hot chicks at a party). I can tell deuschbags or dorks how they can actually have some game over some fairly nice hatchas if they don't screw it up. This is by watching deuschbags actually win some game and sit back wondering what kind of crazy ass shit they said to them to even have girls talking to them. This book is not intended to make anyone in these positions feel better because I am the person that's going to say I don't give a shit and there are certain ways to get girls unless you have my problem which is the 100 year old method of **cockblocking** and there is no sure way to exceed this unless you have other help like good looks (I am the best look-ing guy ever by the way), money, or keep your past girls hidden as to many girls tend to hate other girls (super run on sentence). The reason that I am not set out to make anyone feel better is because no one deserves it if they are reading this book. I do not feel better to watch officers use disrespect against hard working college students or parents to treat the innocent drinkers like a criminal. If the teenager treats the officer badly then he or she deserves the way that the officer treats them. For me to say that officers are disrespectful means that I am also say-ing that teenagers are many times disrespectful to officers. (Now back on the other subject). I can tell you certain things that improve your game like for an example most girls fantasize about older movie stars that look good on camera and have something that others don't. My example will be to act more mature while you are drinking or make them see that you do what others don't in your age group. Some things could include the ability to buy from a liquor store or to go bar hopping. If this is what they want then that is what has to be done to snag hatchas. Although buying alcohol is a very easy task to accomplish, but a lot of times would not even be necessary. That is only if you have no game and you are retarded. Although I don't want to screw it up for the ones who already buy alco-hol so I will wait because I know ten very effective ways and parents will hurt me if I tell their kids. Go to bars, brag about the fun times that you guys have in these places, but not to much because this is the kind of stuff that girls will want to be around, but for some crazy ass reason they always want the guy that seems older. Do not brag about seeming older too much because you will seem like someone who is full of them self. Since you were already planning on drinking and if anything happens, the person who takes responsibility for it always looks older. Smoking cigarettes does not make you look older, and neither does throwing up, but you should be very careful because other guys at parties will find it entertaining to watch this and laugh at you. I know that when I see someone who could not manage how much they drink makes me laugh. I always know when to cut myself off and it comes with being responsible with alcohol. Remember to keep that in mind because not being responsible is why alcohol became illegal for teenagers in the first place. Now the flaw to this example for you people who screw things up is to stay on top, don't just let people call you to just go buy them alcohol (minors buying alcohol for minors is not a crime that I am aware of as it stands), but make them want to hang out. Remember though, I am not telling minors to drink, but for the ones that were already going to drink need to be responsible. If this is not for a sexual reason, then it is for something else. If you do happen to take on something like this, then also be the one who regulates it responsibly. Do not allow people to drink and drive or to drink themselves to a dangerous level. These are the reasons why it is illegal for teenagers to drink (I know that is repeated), but I believe if you can prove that you are responsible enough, then it should not matter. Most other countries share this thought and so do I. There are many ways to go about this, Get to where people look up to you for something like staying in touch with others to always no where a party is, or read up on sports and pretend like you know a lot about them. There are hundreds of ways to improve your game and I have many more examples. For all you crazy ass pretty boys reading this then get rid of the book cause you don't need it, unless you just want to hear a few funny stories that I enjoy telling which I also have most on film, and if I ever get a chance will put the movie out when they can be shortened into a better film with all the stupid shit cut out (awesome run on sentence). I also have a portion of the book that I will label shit talkers and bitch slappers, but I won't because I am lazy. That portion will tell you that if someone is talking trash to you then let it go, unless they get in your face and then you beat their ass no matter what the future holds. If you do not understand the context of the second part, it does not actually speak of slapping girls (if you did, sorry for not putting it in stupid person form). But for example I would like to preach that even though you could look good in front of a bunch of people by beating the hell out of someone talking trash to you, it may hold more bars in the future and put more strain on your game than you think. If they are in your house and you so happen to put them out in a way that's not so violent as I would say and then you tell them to not ever come back, then they will still probably slash your tires or do something bad, but you have to look at things in two tenses. (Present and future at the same time.) Do you want police there and to deal with more rivalry in the future or to look more mature in the process and just handle it like an adult? I am not saying that fighting is bad, but a lot of times just not necessary. When I see people handle something verbally and then they get pissed afterwards is when I tend to see more girls follow the person to make them feel better (always a plus over someone who the girls do not want to punch them in the face from a temper type reflex because they just so happen to be in an unhappy time of their life). Fighting at parties should be avoided because it is not worth it in the long run. Other things that I will talk about are the minorities at parties or in friendships, because they can be special also and it may take other forms of gaining friendships, but if you do not share a lot in common in the first place then don't waste your time trying to be friends. My favorite example is E (short three times for Elbert, lol). Elbert is the only friend that I have right now that I hangout with that is black. I am just as racist as the rest of the world and believe me I will say it, but I am just the same way to most people that are white like me and I hate white people just as much as any race. If your in a Klan then don't read this book cause if the person is my friend whether black or white I will give them the same amount of respect regardless unless they piss me off, but still that would work even if they were white or black. Anyways E is my friend and I will treat him the same as any friend. I will loan him money (although I think I owe him money for a beer right now) if he needs, just like he has loaned me money, I will step in and help him if someone is treating him bad, which I hope he would do the same for me, or go visit him if he's really sick, but my point is that being racist in college and high school will not work very well whether you want it to or not. If you do happen to be racist and you just so happen to throw a party and a black or white person shows up depending on the minority situation, then leave them the hell alone, and let them have fun. Do not go around saying that they will steal shit, and invite their friends. I have been a part of many keggers that me and my friends have thrown with over hundreds of people at single parties (yes I am sure you've been to a bigger one), but the point is that you should treat everyone the same. Most people go to parties for fun and the ones that do mess stuff up are from all races. I am not being sentimental about this because we have thrown parties before and done this, but it's not worth it in the long run. A reason being is that you lose money on what you sale and your party becomes weaker. You want all people and races to know that your parties are the "ah best". Cause I know and my friends know that losing money when you buy around five hundred beers really sucks. So for all you people that are wanting to throw a one race party then look into that section for things like dealing with your guests and the ones that weren't really invited at all (cops).

Alright well that's enough blabbering and I hope your attention was caught so far because this book is written by a group of teenager's (not just me) experiences and I have ideas for taking it to the next level in the future. When I am done with this book then I will want to set up more for other people's thoughts and stories. I will want to create more with stories that are sent to me in the future and allow others to share their thoughts and videos on what college parties, high school parties, and just whatever is like from state to state, cause I want proof that other states party harder than Arkansas and that's right I say Arkansas is a good match unless I can be proven wrong by some stuff (rival run-on). I have no where for these items to be sent, but in the future it will be by the internet or mail. I am just starting the book off and in my spare time setting up an internet site that allows for stuff to be sent in and if it sucks I will burn it, but if its good and I hope its funnier than my stories or whatever so that I can have great shit to laugh at and publish in a video in the future (great run-on). Maybe send in your stories of laws that you found out about at parties the hard way. My best example is that we had more protection than we thought at a party that had a crowd that was out of control and I will tell you more later on or you can just skip to that part if you want. My main point of this entire book is that you do not learn shit about life unless you are around a good amount of people. Let's say you hook up with a kinda nice hatcha (hot chick) at a party for a while. Someone who has not been around that kind of shit before may think that the girl loves him or someone who has only hooked up sober. I believe we all know what I will say next. That's when I would like to step in and well just slap the shit out of him. A party is like Las Vegas and what happens at the party stays at the party. In a situation like this, you get the girls number and don't call for at least a week unless its spring break and then you call as soon as you sober up or start drinking again, but the point is that if she likes you then she will call you and want to do something that's not at a party and then you know it is special. Most people already knew that, but believe me because some readers I guarantee did not know that. Do not try to know how a girl thinks because you can't (believe me I know), but do not hound them when something happens because no matter how you do it, it will still come off as a sloppy approach. Oops I got off subject and if you read this far then you will know I can't stay on subject for shit and I am kind of lazy when it comes to writing and I think it looks more like a teenager wrote it if I just leave it this way. Am I talking about being rebellious to writing or being unique with words? I am tired of writing this little interlude, pre write, or what ever the hell you want to call it.

I will tell you of some of the other subjects I have decided to include on what I think about certain things like the police, drugs, girls (especially ho's), jocks, stoners, rich kids, and fraternities, keggers, BYOB, dealing with parents, and which laws I do not like or understand. This book is to also help parents deal with some normal teenage issues that I have thought really hard about on ways for a teenager and their parents to come to some agreement on. These things include drinking, curfews, drugs (certain ones, but covering both sides like putting a stop to it and allowing it), and a few other things. I went through a lot of trouble to visit schools in my spare time to learn what people are like from school to school (that was not the original plan though). Is the government correct, am I correct, who is correct? I am not out to say that the rules for teenage drinking are wrong and I am not saying that I am right. This is talking about the controversial portions of teenage drinking with a twist. There is no right or wrong to me, but the points that I make on both sides to the issue are important to me and they should be to you also.

To The Parents

I will start off by saying that I am not a parent and will not be one for a while. I can not tell you how to handle your kids and will not even begin to try since all parents are crazy (don't get mad because you are, but teenagers are crazy too) (Two crazies do not make a normal person). Some make more sense than others and some are just whacked out of their minds from being teenagers. Teenagers do not make a whole lot of sense either and especially if they've been drinking because I sure as hell know that I don't. This portion is to just add some suggestions into mind for when some of the normal incidents of partying take place in your family. You have probably had to deal with either drugs, alcohol, sneaking out, bad grades, or just wanting to stay out later. I guarantee you that your child has said something like my best friends get to do it, or they threaten you with something about themselves like dropping out of school or whatever so they can continue having fun. Do not use that as your reason to let them do something (hold true to your real reasons, but allow them to talk because their reasons may be better than yours. Don't ignore your child's reasons for something unless they make no sense, and then smack them in the face for being stupid.) If they want to stay out and go to a party then let them try it. If they come home trashed and your not happy with it then don't let them do it again. What's to hurt that they experienced some alcohol. I mean to be serious about that statement. If you look at it in my viewpoint of being 18 and not being allowed to drink yet, then try to understand these next few statements. Well I checked a global law age requirement web page and you can too, that out of 60 random countries selected, there were only 3 that required for a 21 year old to consume alcohol (most of the world agrees the same except for the U.S. which has only been a parent to citizens for a short time compared to other countries). What is so special about being 21 to consume alcohol? Research shows nothing extraordinary has happened to people that are between 18 and 21 that is that bad compared to people who drink that are 21 (the physical reasons like health in proportions to the same person at a younger age). The amounts of kids between 18 and 21 that drink is the same as it would be if it was to be legal and I promise that this is true through my observations. It is way too easy for a child to get their hands on alcohol (someone buys for them, takes it from home, buys themselves, steals it or whatever). When I see people I know that do not drink that are my age, it is not because it is illegal or that they cant get it, but that they don't like it. I am not saying this law is stupid and that I don't like people who enforce it, but I am just saying that I do not understand where they are coming from on it. I will have just as good a comeback as anything that they want to throw at me for a reason and I will throw comebacks at myself in the book for fun and practice. I hit these issues from both sides to allow controversy within my book. I am not for or against teenage drinking because I do not care if it is legal or not. I am not saying these things to speak of suggested changes in laws, but mainly to show errors that are made through blaming teenagers. (Back on to subject) The U.S. went so long on having 18 as an age requirement for alcohol before they changed it. I have voted this year, and I am fixing to enter college if all goes well, and I am responsible for any crime that I do (**NOT MY PARENTS**) although I do not plan on committing any crimes. The best part to this is that I am old enough to fight for my country as everyone already knows, but cannot buy alcohol. Well, enough of that and if your child decides that he or she is going to drink then that's the end of it. You will not stop them. You may be able to temporarily put it on hold, but if they enjoy it then it will continue to happen. Even if you send them off to a catholic school located on top of a cloud somewhere will still not stop this. Schools like that are the absolute worst about this stuff and the only reason that a teenager wants to come back when sent to one of these schools is because there is no girls or guys present. If you still do not want your child to drink then that's fine. You should work it out in a different way than trying to force them because they are just as strong mentally on fighting for their beliefs as you are and they could be like their parents and listen to the argument, but ignore what's said. Many parents want to say what they think to their kids, but do not listen to how their child feels about it (this was the case with my parents for a while). People will not make fun of him or her for not drinking and they will not put their heads in a toilet. I do not believe that peer pressure happens as much as it is said by some people because most people could care less if one of their friends does not like to drink. They will probably even be seen by one of their friends as a stronger group member for being the one out of the group that stands up to it, but it is usually for a different reason than being illegal for them. If your child wants to do something else then that is something you should think about more. The things I am talking about are staying out later, or my favorite which is going on a road trip without a 39 year old adult to chaperone. The first one and this one will always happen first which is wanting to stay out past their parents bedtime or even staying out past your cities curfew. You do not have to let this happen all the time, but this will make them a lot happier and easier to deal with than drinking. Also if you do not let them out past curfew every once and a while then you will have a problem with your child sneaking out (trust me either way they will go out when they want, but only one way lets you know when) (also that is regardless of what their punishment is unless you tie them down which is kind of funny). You could either know when they are out or not, which means that if you just let them out some times then you will know that they are out and you will not get a wake up call from the police (that was probably a bad run on sentence and I think it repeated another previous sentence). If a parent does not want a drunken teenager then he or she should do the smart thing and not enter the house drunk (that's what a sleep over can be for). When you ask that the person does not come in after your set time or house curfew which to me doesn't make too much sense. The reason is that you do not get bothered by someone coming in the house while you're sleeping. Unless your floor sucks and makes noise or my favorite which is dogs that attack you entering your house (my problem). Your child is responsible enough to handle this task. You may say things to your child like what business does a teenager have being out at 1 in the morning, or there's only drunks and cops out that late. That's true, but who cares what's out there, or what time it is because teenagers are like vampires. They sleep through the day and go out at night. If the driver has not been drinking, then there is little harm to be done. This is when bowling allies are open, Concerts are over, or my favorite which is strip clubs that drain every penny you have in one night (I hate strip clubs because I get peer pressured out of all my money from naked girls) (Just because a teenager is out past midnight does not mean that they are doing bad things). If your child is out drinking all night and sneaks in to the house while your sleeping. You will still know if they were out drinking that night because something will lead back. You will smell it coming off them, their car, or someone will tell you the next day. It cannot be hidden from a parent on the drinking part and should not have to be, but the only reason is because you did it when you were younger. I would be concerned to find out that my child drove home drunk and I would tell them to call me next time. Americans used to have freedoms of governing their children how they wanted, but now most act like robots working for the government. My point is that turning your head the other way a few times will not force your teenager to hit a tree at 120 mph after tons of alcohol unless they had emotional problems, even without the alcohol). This has happened, but cannot show for all teenagers because it would not work with an adult this way. If he or she gets out of control, grades drop, gets into fights, gets arrested, drinks and drives, then you should deal with it, but not harmless drinking in a responsible manner. This is also the same symptoms that adults have and do not even try to say the numbers are the same even though adults drink more through percents of the population. Adults have ways of dealing with this also, but they are not stopped before any drinks are consumed like teenagers are. Your child may not even be peer pressured into drinking. If you are completely determined to find out whom to blame for drinking then start with whoever makes it or advertises it. They rub in your child's face of how good it tastes and most of all how fun it is. Hell they even sponsor race car drivers which I find kind of funny, seeing as how their cars run on a type of alcohol sometimes and they used to spray them with champagne afterwards and then others say "don't drink and drive but we support this type of high speed driving". If you believe that these things cannot be stopped then maybe allowing your teenagers to play in the house would not be such a bad idea. It can be regulated, monitored, and most of all doesn't involve your child driving home late at night. Do not stick your hand in a lion's mouth after someone, unless they can be saved. Doesn't make any sense right, well I just wanted to grab your attention again.

I would like to include a plea, or some type of asking to parents that they just allow their kids to live their lives like it is the only form of life they will receive. It's to short to allow for many years of not enjoying every state of mind possible. Obviously it is your decision on how your kids are raised and will be the same when your child raises their own. Without living life to the fullest, and even if you strongly support afterlife, or whatever the hell you believe in, then still do not waste it with any dull moment. I personally believe that most parents will read this book and end up not changing a thing that my claims state and go back to their regular lives. There is nothing you can do to change a mother's mind that she was set on before you came along (speaking to the teenager). No matter how much debating, fighting, or lying you do then there is still going to be a loss on your side to the parent.

Your child will always try to push back your punishments when the rules are broken. Trust me because I did it every time and it always had some effect, but never completely worked. Parents are much stronger when they feel the safety of their child is at risk. The problem is showing your parents that you are safe about drinking and proving this.

Now I would like to talk about why I have decided to bitch about drinking alcohol even though it poses no challenge to me going to get or having in my possession. I do not even get carded at a lot of places I go. I am too confident for it to show too easy that I am underage and it is not like I would walk in as a teenager (hint, hint). Okay the reason is that I enjoy alcohol very much and in multiple ways. The main and biggest reason is its effect that everyone already knows about. I like to sit around and talk with my friends on the weekends. Most of my friends are in the college age bracket and most are students. Besides this is where focus comes in and I enjoy focusing on stuff that we are talking about after having a few beers. We do not get into rowdy fights often and if it happens, I also believe it would have happened without the alcohol because it has. The other reason is that I am kind of a nerd with alcohol. I have trouble buying the same type twice and the reason is that I like to learn as much as possible about things that are a part of my life, even if it's a very small part. I classify beers that I have tried, stuff like where they come from and what kinds of customs are associated with them. Just like how bartending is a fun job for anyone who even remotely likes alcohol. They learn to make different drinks and what kinds of people enjoy certain ones. Usually I try not to just grab a 30 pack and see how quick they disappear although anyone who drinks at all has done this or tried. I could care less if I did decide to drink one night or if it doesn't happen at all for the whole year. Kids do not go crazy when they see it (hopefully, unless you sheltered your kids which are always the weird ones). It's already too easy for a person to get alcohol and they are used to it enough to where it's a normal substance to them and they do not have to have it as soon as they see it. Usually kids have someone buy it for them. For me I believe that if I can't go and buy it without some minor scheme then I shouldn't need it, but this is only because it is illegal which is not why I drink it at all. So many kids drink now a day that it might be easier to regulate if they could buy it. I think sixteen would be a little young and a person driving after one and half to two beers at this age would make a difference to someone being 18 (yes someone who is 21 would drive better after a few beers, but it is not the case because someone who is 23 would drive better than a 21 year old would). The fact that you can have up to a certain amount if you are 21 and still drive legally does make sense to me because of the amount of driving experience they have. This amount of alcohol would not affect an 18 year old anymore than if that same person was to be 21. The amounts allowed for adults legally to drive are around one beer so it should not affect a teenager driving with one beer if it is not going to intoxicate them. If any teenager says that they become intoxicated from one beer, then they are bullshitting. This should not be a reason for the set age because kids hang out in larger groups than older people. Larger group's means that having a designated driver would be a little easier to acquire because you take turns with more people. My biggest point with the way things are with your children is that the government actually makes drinking a little more dangerous for them due to the ways that they are forced to consume alcohol when they choose to. I have many great examples for this. Your child cannot be in public while drinking because of laws. Therefore he or she will have to drink in parks, houses while the folks are gone, or at parties. These environments are not set well enough for the person to be cut off in time if it is needed. Think about if your child was aloud to go to bars and drink. They would not get alcohol poisoning as easily because bartenders are usually trained a little to know when to cut off someone through nice little signs they watch for. Your child would also have a much easier time getting a cab from a bar than some of the teenage spots used now. I personally know that teenagers may choose to all go to one park or to drink in large groups because they think that the more people that are there would increase their chances of not all being arrested at one time for drinking. They are in fact forced to try things like this because of the way certain laws are set. For these circumstances means that there is say a 100 to 300 people all together with no one to regulate and monitor. You can have someone get hurt showing off in a car or a big fight breaks out, and just many types of dangerous incidents that could happen. People speaking for the government may say that if they would have been older then that would not have happened in a situation like that. Well, if they say that, it is bullshit because they would act the same way if there was no one to stop them because I have seen people of those ages act this way. The only reason it looks like they act more mature is that they drink in public sometimes instead of private and there is someone hired around them to beat their ass for acting this way. They become adaptive to how they are forced to act and it sits with them in other places. This is why less adults show the immature characteristics with alcohol. Teenagers would do the same if the settings could be matched for them. Five kids getting drunk in a house by themselves are not going to act that much different than people that are a little older. Alcohol being legal to people of the age that I speak of will pose other safe roles, also. Let's say that you have a group of five people at a house and they are all 18 years old. If they decide to have sex then the government has no problem with that (I am assuming it's male and female), but they can't drink. Let's also just assume that for some god awful reason that they can't get a hold of alcohol (which I really cannot imagine). They want to have a fun night playing video games, talking, or maybe order some food. Well since they can't get alcohol then they might decide to call a dealer and every kid knows one whether you want to or not and they will buy some drugs cause they can't go buy alcohol, but want to have a little fun. I am not saying extreme types of drugs, but maybe just cannabis. Well this is the case with a lot of people wanting to just let go and relax on the weekend. We are old enough to live on our own but we can't drink. Kids go to school so much in the year, and do not even get paid for it. Some work jobs making hardly any money for the crazy amount of work they do and they deserve to unwind. Kids take on so much more responsibility than they are given credit for, which just pisses me off. I hold strong arguments about drinking and if I was twenty one then I would not have as much reason to want to talk about this, but I would still believe the same things with the bottom of my heart. I am so close to being 21 that it really doesn't make a difference whether I say these things because in a blink of an eye I will be old enough. For everyone who turns 18 is just confused about why they can't drink. We lose large portions of our money to the government that we stake our lives on, stand behind, and pay for, but we get so little in return for what we can do to ourselves to celebrate our lives. It is illegal to kill yourself although that can never be enforced. But this law was written by the same people that write laws about drinking. Do they really have strong enough reasons for all their laws that they make or are they just based on statistics that anyone could have written? Does it bother the people on the committees for the stuff they pass, No (they are not affected by it because if they were, then they simply would not vote for it). House of Representatives, Senate, and Congress, all these people could care less about the taxes or rules that they impose, or who this stuff effects or who gets to drink. I could write all day about wasted money, ridiculous laws, or laws targeted to certain people. I am only choosing to write about the ones presently affecting me right now. I have heard so many things that piss me off that has been said about kids and drinking. They make it seem like it's so bad for us. I am at the stage in my life where I will not grow much more the rest of my life and actually I was told to lose some weight. I will not get any taller, but maybe just a little wider. If you tell me that it is damaging my body more because of my age then I will indeed slap you in the face. I am just as mature as I will be 40 years from now although I will be a little wiser or dead. When I see someone get into a fight, I will still break it up (unless boxing or something) just like an older person would. I will not support buying really young people alcohol because I feel that there are more dangers to that. I believe that if you are not old enough to manage your life on your own then you should not be aloud to drink without someone responsible around you. There is not a whole lot more difference to someone between 18 and 21 drinking and I am going to continue to restate that off and on. So many incidents happen in college from drinking because they are finally away from home and it has become easier for them to purchase or has just entered their life. This is when people do stupid things and once again is not regulated. If they had been aloud to start drinking when they were living with their parents then it would not have had as bad an effect when they hit college. The reason for this is very obvious and that it would not be something new or appealing to them when they were away from their parents. Parents would still get pissed if their child drank too much even if it were legal for their child at that age. A parent can regulate what their child does and does not do a hundred times better than the government can because they are in the persons life much more than an officer of the law (Hopefully). My next big argument would be that if a child wanted to throw a big party with alcohol being legal for their ages then it could be managed better. They could get a cheap permit for selling beer, hire some security, advertise it, and order some type of transportation for people willing to accept it and pay for it through the money made on their party (kick ass run-on, several points made). Then you wouldn't have broken stuff because of security, drunk driving, and beer would be sold with a permit. This would make everyone happy and for a safe party instead of one thrown in secret with a bad outcome. The government would make money off this through taxes and so would other companies instead of a child who is forced to throw a party in secret that would have the police called and stuff gets broken or people get arrested for wanting to have a good time. Your child has things that he or she wants to celebrate and for me it's got a few walls around it. My school has had two years of state championships in football and all parties that are thrown are secrets due to being illegal because there is alcohol present. These people have more to celebrate than any adult and did not even get paid for these accomplishments like an adult would. It's always hilarious to watch teenagers getting drunk at parties in the movies and no one says anything about it until their child is at one. This is going to happen whether it is a felony to throw a party or just a small ticket. We cannot call for transportation afterwards or for security because it would make the party as obvious as a neon sign as far as people trying to crash the party. I am going to live every minute of my life to the fullest and nothing will stop that. I refuse to commit crimes like stealing, murder, or rape because jail would be a huge portion of my one shot at life being ruined. I would like to have experience knowing as many people as possible, experiencing different viewpoints, and different ways to have fun like: parties, museums, theme parks, other countries, and anything I can think of because life is so short. I am not going to let the government stop me on anything I want to do because I will regret it when I am closer to death and feel I should have had more fun in life. Your child feels the same way and too much is being asked out of their lives. I enjoy learning and that's what keeps me in school. It is not because I know it is what I will use to survive later, but because these things interest me and allows me to put up a better fight against stuff in the future that I want to help change. I just want to speak how I feel and if this book changes the way the whole world thinks then fine, or if no single person likes it then fine, also. This book is only being written by me for the purpose that I can read it later feeling that I have put up a good argument (I Hope), even if it never goes anywhere. This book is just me wanting to have these things said and put aside. If it turns out to suck really bad then that's fine and I won't write any more books, but I enjoy reading this because all my thoughts on this subject are compressed into a short summary. I do not constantly talk like this in public and I have never found myself talking about these things with my friends. I am not the kind of person who talks about what I think the government does wrong all the time because it doesn't bother me much unless it is rubbed in my face real bad like drinking alcohol. This book is the only thing I have said written or verbally about what I think. When I am with friends then everything I talk about is normal. I am not a protesting type person because I like to approach things in a more professional way. I have not graduated college, received an important job, so there is nothing about me that would make me a professional at anything (although I am still a student so that should make some sense.) I have no background in writing to make a great author except exceptional grades in English classes and really high A.C.T. Assessment scores in English and Grammar. I am just a kid who enjoys writing and would like to write a book on what I have learned through my own personal research. I am not a lawyer that knows all the laws, and I am not a parent (Thank god). With all this said then please read my book out of interest and don't use it to argue with your children or parents unless you feel it is necessary. I just want to allow people to feel better about stuff in their life and for teenagers to not feel bad about drinking if you were responsible in the process. Do not feel horrible that you have decided to drink for celebrating something because to me is what can relieve stress or tension and in turn make you feel better. Your kids are not stupid, although some are definitely smarter than others. This section was for parents to read mainly and the rest of the book is quite different. I am now going to start with the first part of my book.

Miscellaneous Information on Drinking

Drinking is a part of many cultures and demonstrates many rituals from country to country. America has more drinking cultures than any other country. The reason for this is that the U.S. was founded on other cultures or from other countries and immigrants coming to this country. All of these cultures have supplied us with a large mixture of different types of drinking methods. Although for a country to limit the age of drinking, but represent other cultures that teach it at these forbidden ages shows confusion in a worldwide sense. I believe that this age restriction of the U.S. has been created out of fear of a young person's health and the health to the ones around them during a state of intoxication. Teenagers have prepared their entire lives for the life of college or through their chosen careers up to that point. But, the one thing that they have not been allowed to prepare for and the most dangerous to their health are what they will have to learn on their own. I would like to explain that it is more dangerous for a person to not be able to drink legally as a teenager. I am not going to give an age on what I think, because regardless of what I think will not change the age laws. I will say that allowing a sixteen year old to drink beer in a bar and an 18 year old to purchase hard liquor on their own does seem to work pretty well for other countries. This allows the adults to regulate when the person should not drink any more. This also gives the teenager two years experience under adult supervision on drinking before they are allowed to purchase and drink on their own. That is a big reason for why drinking works better in other countries for teenagers and makes it safer also. This is due to not being able to stop teenagers completely from drinking and approaching it with better methods. I have learned this through my observations and research while in many European countries. I have observed that if a country can make alcohol seem like it is not a big deal, then it is not treated like it is a big deal or abused. What I mean by that is that when your child drinks illegally means that they will take advantage of it no matter where they happen to be, due to not knowing exactly when it will happen again. Many teenagers drink every chance they get because they cannot choose a lot of times when it would be better or when it would not affect anything. Adults can drink whenever they want. They have the ability to wait until their work will not be affected or when it is their spare time. Some teenagers may have to just go with the time that is given to them instead of it being a time that would not affect school or work. They want the full effect possible from alcohol because it is illegal and they may not get to do it again for a while. For adults this means that they can have it whenever they want and do not have to go crazy with it because they can sit and enjoy alcohol by taking their time. If a teenager could buy alcohol then they would no longer view it as such a big deal to have in their possession. This would also allow them to drink less knowing that fewer people could care less if they choose to drink. Teenagers would no longer feel any better than the ones who don't drink because the others would be seen as the ones who choose not too instead of being afraid of getting in trouble. What I observed in Europe is that the teenagers across the seas have learned to deal with it safely so that it will not become illegal to them. Many people who are against teenage drinking might say that it would be easier to just keep avoiding it and to not try and legalize it for a lower age. What could be better at research than to try it? Some people might say that what I have just said is bullshit, but in the next few paragraphs will allow me to explain very tempting reasons to back it up.

Everyone knows that teenagers are strong mentally and physically. A teenager performs athletics that are not that much different than it would be if they were an older adult. Also a teen demonstrates levels of education (if they are normal) that can be just as hard as and even harder than a lot of college classes. They show much responsibility through managing jobs, sometimes utilities and rent, school, and all at the same time. What we receive in return for this is not equal to the amount of responsibility that we take on. By stating on how strong we are as teenagers would show that if we decide to do something means that there is no stopping it and even if we believe in it.

(Example) Your child has been caught drinking by a law enforcement officer. He or she has also been given a citation for this drinking and you have also found out that there would have driving involved if they were not caught. You have also found out that your child has been drinking every weekend and driving home and trying to act normal when they come in. Well as a parent you would be pissed at them and try to do something to stop it. I believe that the way you think of dealing with this should be altered a little. What if you had allowed them to do all this drinking at home under your supervision to start with? If your child had been able to do this instead, then I have found some ways that would work in a more secure way. First, the driving part would be completely eliminated. Your child would drink under the parent's supervision for the first several times instead of away from them at a party for the first time (which is more dangerous?). They would not be afraid to call you instead of driving in the future, fearing punishment. Your child could learn from the parent themselves about how to deal with certain situations. When your child enters the world to drink with their friends whom I assure you will happen at some point and will allow them the advantages over other people of the same age. Your child is not going to freak out when they see alcohol and immediately want every drop like the other kids. They will treat alcohol like an adult and use it wisely by remembering that it is not the only thing in the room with them. The reasons for this would be that you were there to cut them off when it was needed or to give their friends a ride home instead of them driving while they learned to deal with alcohol. They will be more use to this and it will settle into their heads before they find themselves behind the wheel of a car. I say these things from my heart that is true in every since. I have known people to die from drinking and they were all sheltered people who their parents feared alcohol. The person would go crazy when they finally got out of their sheltered house and these are irresponsible teenagers not worthy of drinking (a lot of times). These kids thought too much of alcohol and drank too much since it was very new to them and they went crazy with it. It must be treated like drinking is not a big deal in the sense that you are responsible about it. Why not teach your kids or as teenagers reading yourself about alcohol in a responsible manner. I am not saying that drinking less is an always or that drinking a lot should never happen. How is a teenager supposed to go about drinking and plan ahead by knowing exactly how it will happen? An adult has the advantage to helping them from making mistakes. For a child there is no one there to monitor it and regulate during the drinking. Adults go to bars where they are monitored and regulated while drinking. Obviously they drink at home, but through both scenes of the drinking teaches them to use it in a mature way. The only way that teenagers are able to drink is to get it in quantities for the whole night and meet with their friends of the same age. They cannot go to a bar and drink and see how most act around it. They are forced to try the intoxication together for the first time and it moves on from there. If your child was able to go to a bar and drink then most would act like the ones around them at the bar. Of course some stupid ass girl or guy is going to act like a fool in the bar out of a group that is drinking for the first time. But, there would also be someone there to tell them to shut the hell up and either remove them from the bar or cut them off unlike this happening in a park. This would teach someone real quick that this is not acceptable with drinking. As far as the drinking and driving goes is a little harder to teach a teenager. There are way too many adults that do this to show that it is so wrong for a teenager. Some teenagers even drink to be more like an adult, but I believe the driving part is for a different reason unless they are really stupid. Bars sometimes even offer adult's free rides home when they purchase enough alcohol and the adults are being babied, but children are forced into dangerous situations when they choose to drink. No one offers them the safeties that adults have and basically says for all the blind people to know is, that kids deserve the dangers that they get for drinking. This is what allows them to say what the dangers of underage drinking are. But they do not tell you that the government has created them to be able to say this.

If the U.S. would make the age restriction a little more convenient for a few more ages could in fact change a few observations. There is no way to stop a teenager from drinking and they have too much to fight for to be allowed to drink. As a teenager I am expected of my country to be there if I am needed to fight others in time of war. I take on the responsibility knowing that I will die for my country if I am asked, but I cannot have a drink. I hate using this statement as my defense because I hear this from many other people and it is definitely a little redundant, but also very true. I also spend every single weekday getting up early in the morning and heading to school. As soon as I leave school is when I rush over to my job where I work till nighttime. After work is when I have just enough time to eat dinner and do my homework just so that I can start over the next day. On Saturday is when I get up early and work a full shift. How can someone tell me that I am two young to drink when I take on more responsibility than most adults I see today? An adult works a normal shift everyday and they have more right to drink than I do, but they do less (doesn't make sense). I pay more taxes out of my paychecks than adults do because I am a student. I give more percentages of taxes to the government for hard work that I get paid less for than an adult does. I believe that I should have the right to have a drink on the one day of the week that I do not work my ass off all day. This would be Saturday night and then on Sunday is when I wake up and study all day for the next week. Do I deserve to be able to unwind and just relax one night of the week with a few beers, maybe more, but shouldn't I also have the right to make some decisions like this? I am old enough to vote on the people that make these laws, old enough to live on my own and make any other decision that an adult would. I can buy the most damaging substance on the planet (tobacco, but I choose not to). I have proven my strength against the strongest peer pressure by quitting tobacco for a very long time now. I make all life changing decisions about my life. I am old enough to get married, have sex, travel to other countries, **be a father**, and represent myself in a court of law. Yet, I still cannot go to a bar, sit down with my college buddies and have a drink. I can grow a beard and some people say I look thirty and many liquor stores do not even card me because of it, but legally I am not supposed to do that. I give you every reason that makes me an adult in the above sentences, but I cannot drink. There is no physical difference between myself in a few years and myself right now. I am an adult that cannot drink is what I am. I feel very passionate about not being able to drink. If you have decided to read this book, then by now you are probably thinking that I am an alcoholic. I can go as long as it takes without alcohol and there are months that I choose not to drink and some months I choose to drink a lot. At the point that this exact sentence was written, I went an entire month without a single sip of alcohol (just did not feel like drinking). You are also wondering why I keep whining just about alcohol. The reason is that I feel that if I can not cover an entire book worth of facts, and compelling statements, then I would not feel passionately enough about the subject that I want to change. I read about too many accidents with alcohol and it continues to happen more and more. Obviously, trying to stop it is not going to work. But, maybe allowing it with better ways to monitor it would work better. If I can write an entire book with nothing in it but persuading sentences on a single subject, then maybe someone will take me seriously. Plus the hundreds and hundreds of dollars that I spent to get this book published. I am telling people how to save their child's life by teaching them how to drink themselves. If you don't, then they will try to learn it on their own by themselves. This is more dangerous than allowing your child to learn to drink behind your back by thinking that you don't know what's going on. This book is not to change the laws for me because it does not affect me the way that the laws are set right now. I have had drinks in bars, and shopped at every liquor store in my town at least once. I am speaking for all teenagers that just continue to break the laws and accept the punishment. I accept any punishment for my actions, also. I want to see what others think about my theory and see if people can work together to change it. If not by reversing it, then by altering it and letting it stand in a way that allows teenagers to be monitored when they drink, if in public. Alright I would like to now get back on subject.

My next big argument is towards the parents and most of the book has been about half and half on the targets for the reader (between the parents and the teenagers). I am asking you to think on this part and mainly about the dangers of underage drinking. For every danger that you can think of on underage drinking is where I want you to keep thinking about what causes it. Don't look at the teenager, but look even deeper and towards the source of the problem. An example is going to be Drinking and driving. Your child or a teenager has chosen to drink and drive home after a party. Most will think it is the teenagers fault and this may be true. Deeper in the situation though will mean that he or she drove because they could not call for a ride without getting in some trouble. Maybe they are afraid that their parents would get mad at them. Would this overlap the fact that your child would not have chosen to drink if he or she knew ahead of time that driving would be involved? A lot of times when a teenager finds out that he is going to drink will happen from a phone call thirty minutes before the drinking starts (that means that someone could be sitting at home and gets invited to a party on the spot.). Someone calls the teenager and says there is a great party and you should come over. Since most teenagers do not get to choose exactly when they drink means that there is a long time between when the person gets to unwind and hang out. If it were legal all the time then the person would show up at the party and would not really care if he or she chose to drink that night, wanting to make sure that they could be safe about knowing that the teenager could wait and drink when there is a designated driver (average run-on). So the true source of this could not be the teenager. Another example that I want you to think about would be who is to blame for a teenager drinking too much and doing something that's not very responsible. A bunch of the time is where this could be the teenager's fault; maybe the teenager was showing off, nobody taught the person when to stop, or they were peer pressured. You must think deeper than that and this could be many things. Commercials of guys slamming beers at incredibly fast rates (I know that people cannot be seen drinking beer in commercials, but the empty cans next to them is a key symbol) may make the person think they can do it also because I sure as hell know I can. Another factor could be that the person hears talk of adults saying how much they drank at a wrestling match, bar, or something. My point here is that teenagers do make mistakes, but sometimes is where it is not completely their fault. If it is not their fault it will still be blamed on them even though they were driven crazy to do this. Fine, whatever, but I do not need an excuse for being caught drinking. If I am caught drinking, then I will take credit for it and accept my ticket or punishment. There is nothing I can do, but if I choose to drink then that will be my excuse. That is the most mature thing I can think of that would involve me and being caught drinking. Once again I will say that there is no stopping a teenager from drinking. If they get out of hand then, there might not be much you can do about it. Adults get out of hand in the same ways that teenagers do, but does alcohol become illegal for adults? Someone may say that all adults do not get out of hand, but when you think about it, neither do all teenagers and I have not found myself in this position.

I would like to retell a story that I have in mind from what I have read on a story on the internet. I have seen two similar stories from the one that I will retell. I read them a long time ago and can't remember where it was, but I hope the writer feels good about his story. It touched my heart to know that this parent cared so much for his child that he performed what I have been suggesting and proved that it can be safe. He broke the laws on allowing teenagers to drink so that he could feel safe for his son that had told him that he would drink on prom night no matter what anyone says to him. The fact that this dad was willing to allow it in his house just like how adults are babied with being able to go to bars. This dad was able to regulate and monitor the drinking of the thirty kids that came to his house that night. When I read this story before and it made me realize how many kids that did not come to this mans house and were forced to drink somewhere else and had to sleep in their cars or drive drunk afterwards to their houses. Those kids could not go to a bar and get a cab home, but had to drink and drive, but were forced through wanting to do what every generation of kids before them did on their prom night. This dad collected car keys and stayed awake to handle the police and show that everything was alright. I did not read of reports of fights, alcohol poisoning, or even girls being taken advantage of. This dad was later arrested for what he did and for all we know saved every kids life at that party. Adults can drink in their houses and at bars with planned out ways of how they will get home. What the hell can a kid do when they decide to drink? They can plan ahead and most do, but cannot plan for a perfect and safe place to do it like adults are allowed to. Teenagers that drink are forced to show more responsibility than an adult. They are forced to drink in places where they do not have their own security, or a staff to monitor their actions (like Parks). I will keep saying this because the government keeps saying things that are only true when put on different weighted scales. Until they can have all situations the same and then trying to run statistics, would make more sense to me. Without that means that there is some type of guessing involved through assuming situations stay the same from teenager to teenager.

My next argument is that most parents that you see take advantage of everything that they are allowed to do. People are allowed to smoke tobacco and drink. Both are taken advantage of by many adults. Who is to say that anyone who drinks and smokes would not accept cannabis if it were legal? Countries that have this herb legal to the public have outstanding numbers of people who do it. Those people in other countries are my brothers and sisters just like you. We are the same people and if this herb were legal in the U.S. would mean that there would be outstanding numbers of people accepting it into their lives. I will admit that I also enjoy the drug, but I am not addicted to it and since this statement I have decided to take a long break from it to prove myself. I will go as long as anyone asks me, and just to prove, but I also think that it should be legal. Plus since this exact statement was written, I have gone about a year from doing the drug and I don't really plan on doing it again (me quitting for the rest of my life is going to prove this, but I will miss it). The reason for me stopping is not that it is illegal; but that I have grown tired of it and that I don't need a replacement for it. This means that I am drug free although it is not really a drug. I have also decided to exercise a lot more. These things that I have done like quitting is to show that I am not out to provide for myself, but for what I believe in. I have nothing against tobacco and cannabis, but I would also like to show that it is not my addiction talking. My subject here is not to persuade anyone on it, but to say that if it were legal would be just as popular as alcohol. I know many teenagers that do this drug because they cannot get their hands on alcohol or that they feel it is safer than alcohol. Adults will do whatever they can get their hands on. My best example is that I visited a bar one time and noticed that absinth was being served. This is a type of poison that I am very certain has laws against it in certain ways and especially being sold in the U.S. I believe it has something to do with being illegal to resale or market in the U.S. Adults were buying the shit out of this stuff and it was because they could get their hands on it and not be arrested. I will not tell the bars name because I am not the one to put a stop to things like this since no one cares what teenagers think. Many adults will just stick to what the government allows because they do not want jail time. This means that they will not fight for the things they like better, because many are afraid. Teenagers a lot of times share the same theory, but what is there for a teenager to unwind on. Salvia, Duster, Gasoline is all things that I see many teenagers doing. I can't stand any of these items, but many kids around my age do this because they can't get alcohol which is much safer in health reasons if they could just be taught to use it in a safe way. What do you believe is worse; an eighteen year old having a few beers or to huff a can of duster and killing like forty trillion brain cells? Although the product duster works great on my keyboard and computer tower, but I do not find it worth huffing, although it is probably great. I just do not care for it.

Teenagers are not perfect and many have bad problems, but it is not enough to imprison all from trying to buy alcohol. The longer that they have to wait for it means the more they will go crazy with it when it enters their life. I will say again that the purpose of this book is not to try and legalize it for people to party, but to change laws for the safety of people. I have already given reasons why and this is not for me to get to drink because making it legal would not change anything for me. I can already buy at any liquor store that I choose and without a fake id. It may include taking a friend to buy it, playing it off, or doing whatever. I have ten ways in my head now that I have used to buy alcohol and they are not just things you say. One of my biggest points that I like to talk about is that the problem with underage drinking is going to get worse and worse as more kids grow up together and more drink together. It is going to be a lot harder for a child to avoid drinking at a party with five hundred people in the future when the party would be like only a hundred people today (populations continue to rise). I am not talking to the government because obviously they do not listen to a god damn word that anyone says to them. I am talking to future parents and future teenagers who I hope to change to realizing how they can teach their kids in a different, but more effective and safer way on drinking. For parents, then I have given many effective ways on treating your child's drinking with both of you being satisfied.

Why do you think that teenagers say that they would rather go to any other country on the planet than the U.S. for Spring Break? This is because any other country believes that it is o.k. for your child to drink as a teenager. There are so many countries that believe it is harmless and it has been that way for more years than the U.S. has even been a country. These other countries are the parents to our country and it is working fine for them, but why the U.S? Why is it so dangerous for a teenager to drink in public in the U.S.? I have even been carded for mouthwash and cough medicine containing alcohol before (I don't think I could physically drink mouthwash without throwing up so why the hell would that be illegal for me). The government is so scared for something that is really none of their business. I will kill myself before the day that I drink either one of those substances above to get drunk. Some kids drink these items to get drunk and it is more dangerous for them to do this than normal alcohol. I would rather be completely sober than to drink something like that. I would drink fermented potatoes strained through an old sock aged into the nastiest alcohol ever before I would drink mouthwash and cough medicine to get drunk. I am not saying I would drink the potato stuff either, but it is ridiculous on how it is treated. You can be arrested as a teenager for drinking one beer and being in public, but an adult can come to a restaurant that I used to work at and drink till he throws up all over his wife (that's pretty funny though). Even if alcohol is never permitted for a teenager and my book never changes a single person's mind will still confuse me on why it is illegal for a teenager to have one beer. Many adults go to a bar or sit down at a restaurant and drink one beer. My dad does this all the time and when we go to a restaurant and eat is when he has a beer with dinner. I can't have a beer, but I can go into the army and fight for my entire family's freedom and all I would get is an education afterwards and money that is no where near the equivalence to a human being's life. It has nothing to do with what I am given personally for a service like that, but the amount of responsibility and courage that I would have to show and when it's all over I still could not buy beer if under twenty one. I can have children, get married, live on my own, and try to raise a family, but not drink. I can tattoo my forehead with millions of triangles, but not drink alcohol. I can pierce every piece of skin on my body, but not drink alcohol. I am to be tried as an adult for every crime that I could possibly commit, but not drink alcohol. I can become a porn star (maybe) and sleep with a million women on film, but not drink alcohol. Do you get my point, because I am tired of naming examples? I actually have friends that I have talked to that have come back from the war in Iraq and Afghanistan and could have died for their country, but could not go and buy beer while being under twenty one and already sent to war in the same lifetime. I hope I have made some sense so far.

What I Think of Police and Underage Drinking

Many people who have had to deal with police from throwing a party, or they got a DUI probably does not like the police very much. I have had to deal with the police quite a few times, and for different reasons. Many will say that the officers do not understand what it is like to be a teenager or to have fun as a teenager. My point is that these people will continue to hate cops, but when something happens to them is when they will also want their services.

I do not hate cops and there will never be a time that I do. Even if they bust your party and send a bunch of your friends to jail or whatever, is still not reason to hate them in general. Yes, it is true that they are trained to be assholes and without acting that way then people would walk all over them. There are many rules that I am completely against and some of the ways that they follow procedure. The officers will tell you stuff sometimes that is not true or treat you really bad with disrespect, but you have to handle stuff in a certain way or they will not take you seriously. Bribing, yelling, and running are all bad ideas and I am strongly against them. Being intoxicated is not as big a deal as most people make it out to be. You will only make it worse by acting crazy. Like I said earlier that out of 60 random countries, that only 3 required that you be 21. I am really not worried about what the government has to say on drinking. There are hundreds of things that I go on that the government says and I do not even question it. When it comes to stuff that involves my life, then they will really have to do some convincing with great reasons to persuade me to live my life the way they say to. I have heard many rumors that I believe are true about being able to drink when you turn 18 if you join the army. If there were more countries that shared the same rules on this subject, then I would possibly consider believing it. Although who cares if you get to drink in the army because if I went to serve my country then I would not drink while in the service. The feeling of being in the army to me would be scary enough that I would want to stay sober at all times for emergency reasons. Police take underage drinking as seriously as anything they come across. Many kids are scared to call cabs, ride the bus, or call their parents after they have been drinking. In return these kids try to drive home without being caught which is even more dangerous to their health. If kids could drink in a bar, then it would show more care on their lives for it to be regulated. There is too many ways for an adult to have a designated ride, but for a child is where they make it seem that if you drink, you will have to drive yourself and that helps them build up the statistics they need to keep it illegal for kids. They promote drinking for people that are 21 and provide every safety precaution to help them with it, but offer nothing to the teenagers who do decide to drink. I have also told in the first part, many examples of how it is more dangerous for the drinking age to be set where it is than the safety it supposedly provides right now. Your kids will drink and that is the end of it unless they choose not to on their own. Would you rather your child drink without the parent knowing and doing whatever or by knowing that they are doing it and to be able to offer help to them when they need it or go a little overboard. I am not talking about rehab or some party school off in the mountains for all boys or girls. I am talking about driving them when needed, or a teenager being able to tell their parent what really went on that night without fear of punishment. If someone's parent were too drink too much at a bar, their child would come and pick them up without bitching about their parent drinking, usually because the main thing with drinking is to just be safe about it. As for a child drinking, then their parent would go crazy to have to come pick their child up for drinking and a lot would say that you are on your own. I would like to respond to the questions of these parents who are bitching about it and if they can convince me with better remarks than the ones I am making myself then I will change the way I think and write a book stating the opposite. Good Luck Though.

As far as the theories on marijuana goes is that I am confused on what to believe. I am told by the government all this stuff about the drug and when I read into it out of personal interest is where the truth is all skewed. I cannot trust the government on stuff anymore and have to learn for myself what I believe is bad and good. I am not going to try to convince anyone about this drug because it just seems pointless trying to state your argument about it. Police treat this drug as if it is a murder weapon. When they see it is when they freak out, draw their guns, and use harsh physical force to put someone into custody. I guess if they were throwing bricks of the drug at them and knocking officers out with it would make this a necessary procedure, but that doesn't happen (It would be a funny episode of COPS though "man throws deadly striking forces of raw cannabis shaped bricks at authorities"). There are not very many adults in public blabbering about the better sides to it right now, but there is a huge amount saying bad stuff about it. When I read into this is where I saw a fifty/fifty margin on good and bad theories towards this drug. Adults do not listen to teenagers no matter how much sense they happen to make on a subject which is why I will not even try to convince parents, but by saying stuff about both sides of it is where I can see what they think on it. They say that cannabis is a gateway drug and there are many commercials about this for prevention. I do not personally think that is true, but if it is then I would agree that it is a satanic substance and would withdraw my statements. They cannot be a hundred percent sure of this though. I would like to say a few things that are skewed about it though. This is not just for marijuana purposes, but to help explain why everything the government says is wrong in some way just like most facts about the drinking ages (This is the only thing I am pissed about even though I do not even drink that much unless celebrating something). This is to show that anything in the general party category has a fact that is all mixed up to persuade people on the laws about it. The first thing that I would like to talk about is that they say that terrorists are funded from buying drugs like marijuana (but buying Gasoline isn't?). I believe this is not true, but even if it was would mean that having it to be grown in the U.S. would stop the support to terrorists. When I look at it like this is where I think to myself of how the government would rather have terrorists funded than to have marijuana legalized. They say that this is bad, but when you look at it from another point of view, then it would actually seem more dangerous the way things are now. I have read many things saying marijuana is safe and the same amount saying it is dangerous. Teenagers try to convince their parents that it is safe so they will leave them alone about it. I am not sure where to start on the subject because just like any other teen, I do not have a medical degree with my own personal research on it. Since I cannot do this, then I would like to make both sides available and through your own reading will show you where your own standing on your decision is. Any police officer has ancestors who used the drug because it has been around for two many years and was legal for quite some time. Most parents that are against this drug are because they know that it can get them in trouble for their child's actions. By me saying that, would give them a great reason to be against it. It is always embarrassing when your family finds out about another family member getting into trouble. Although maybe this would make them a coward if the person is not really against it inside, but stays away from it because the government says no. Although if the drug were to be legal, then would you think the same. Would you care if your family knew that you smoked cannabis if the drug was legal? They say it can cure pains that are really bad and stressful. Well, so do pain medications and I believe that taking them would be worse for you if you used them like someone were to use marijuana, but the pills are still legal. Some of these pills are even classified as synthetic heroine. It is a pill with effects similar to the drug from what I hear and is extremely addictive. Americans say nothing bad or have anything to say about taking it because it is allowed. If a drug or substance is allowed by the **U.S. Government** then the citizens are all for it, but when it is illegal, even if it is cough drops is where people would begin to hate it. Everyone seems to be scared of it, and refuses it. I am not telling anyone to use this stuff against their parents or for parents themselves to use it against their kids. I don't care if you love the drug, or hate it and everyone that does it. I believe that what you choose to do should fall under freedom of speech or there should be an amendment for freedom of personal actions. Wouldn't it be cool for some people if the drug was legalized? Wouldn't it also be cool for some people if they found a way to make the drug extinct? The reason that I talk of this drug particularly is that most people reading this has done the drug. I know that if you have done the drug, then you have your own personal opinions on it. Well what about the people that happen to be the reason for its illegalness but swear they have never done it before. Do you think this is fair that the ones who make this law are the ones who probably could not even identify it? They write laws like this on what a few scientists have told them. The scientists say there is more tar in it then cigarettes and even if that is true does not mean that there are more deadly chemicals. Do the scientists tell them everything they need to make their decisions on these laws? I think the people who research the drug should make this law or the people who have done the drug, but using a fifty/fifty proportion of people still using it and not. I do not talk about drugs like crack because I have never done them. I do not plan on doing the drug because I don't have any family members who have done it, nor do I read that there are good effects to it. Crack may be great, or it may be bad like they say. There is nothing I have read saying that it is good for you. Crack is illegal just like marijuana. There are just as many people saying positive things about marijuana as negative things. So no matter what they say about the drug, it is still going to be different than other drugs. You take all these drugs that are legal and the side effects are like 40 pages long, but you have no concerns for them because they are legal to you. Marijuana on the other hand has fewer side effects than a lot of drugs out there and people are against it just because the government says no. When you think about stuff this way, then you wonder what the real reason for it being illegal is. Is there one big reason for it being illegal, or is it just stuff that is said, but not completely proven. They say that one joint is equal to 20 cigarettes in the amount of tar. They do not tell you anything else. Would you believe something even though they do not give you full detail? What if this was the harshest and craziest type of weed ever invented compared to the lightest type of tobacco that is produced (did they say anything like that when they made that statement to you or that they could prove that this type of weed should be compared with that type of tobacco). This could also be turned the other way making weed worse than they even say it is. My point is that you do not know being the consumer of the information completely enough to make a good decision that everyone is making. Once again, I am not trying to convince you because I know that it doesn't work (Mainly speaking to parents). I will ask for the sake of convincing your parents or child that you will read into it yourself instead of listening to the TV or the government all the time. This is whether you are trying to bring it into your life or remove it, but do not trust the so called facts they tell you about stuff until you believe that they have been honest and given you the full details that you deserve. I have told you both sides of stuff I talk about and unlike the government I would like to see if this works better to persuade people and to read on their own of how they should deal with stuff like underage drinking.

You are probably wondering why I decided to share the few above paragraphs about marijuana. The reason is that at one point in my life I did the drug and enjoyed it. The experience of it should not be hidden, but used to talk about how you feel about it. Since this book I have decided to quit the drug. I am not out to have it legalized or to help get rid of it. I do not care what happens with it. I do believe that some people with disabilities deserve this drug and that it is safer than a lot of other pharmaceutical drugs. I do not personally care if I am around it or not. I believe that if people want something then let them have it. This will eliminate drug dealers making easy money off of it. Two problems solved in one decision. You as the reader probably assumed that I was addicted to the drug because I decided to speak of it in such ways. By giving it up I would like to show you that it means nothing to me. By the time that you read the published form of this book, I will have gone a year and counting without this drug (repeated). I do not care for harmful drugs. This includes pills, heroine, crack, cocaine, LSD, speed, amphetamines, Hallucinogens, Mescaline, Psilocybin, steroids, Viagra, duster, Oxycontin, Opium, Morphine, Benzocaine, Nitrous Oxide (maybe), Nicotine or whatever the hell you want to add to the list. By the way I looked up most of those drugs and I don't even know what a lot of them are. I do not want people to think that I am writing this stuff for myself. I am writing this stuff for informative controversial and competitive research for personal use (That doesn't make sense to me either). I have given up smoking tobacco for a very long time now.

Before the first copy of my book will be published, a year has gone by without tobacco in my life. I quit addictions because I think that is my biggest gift or talent. I would also like to write a book later telling you my strategies for quitting tobacco. I get sick to even look at cigarettes from my method. Once again I do not care what anyone thinks because I am right and you are wrong, even if you say the same thing that I did you will still be wrong. That was a joke for you to laugh at if you didn't catch on.

Throwing a Party Responsibly

If you actually decide to throw a party, then there are a few things I would like to tell you from past experience. By throwing a party then you will also risk a lot depending on if it is at your house, private land, parking lot, or on a sandbar. Some risk a lot and the others risk an extreme amount, but in the end will always be fun no matter what your outcome of the event happens to be. I would like to start off with the classical throw a party while your folks are out of town.

Your parents leave for a weekend vacation and this is the standard plot for thousands of parties. You decide that you are free and you would like to go crazy for the weekend. You've been planning this event for weeks or every since they told you that they were going out of town. If your parents know that you have any friends at all then they will also know that there will be people at your house while they are gone (but maybe not a hundred or more). What they don't know and pray to god is that there will be no party and I guarantee you that you were warned if you throw one by your parents. This party will either be good and the only thing that sucks about it will be the cleanup or something really bad will happen. This could be that you screw up and all your friends go to jail and you get a massive ticket, or my favorite which is your parents come home early (surprise). In my opinion, I would rather deal with the cops because my friends and I do a good job of handling this, but if you still live with your folks then there is no way in hell that you will be able to send them away when they show up. Especially when they see cars as far as their eyes can see facing their own house. Other side effects of parties like this could be excessive trash that fills up your dumpster and all your neighbors' dumpsters which was a problem of parties I have been to in the past. The other problems are that stuff gets broken (lamps, shades, glass, walls, and even trees, lol) because nothing at a party is sacred. Little things that you should also watch for is who to cut off on drinking and watch them because they will throw up and it's always the worst place for it. I have even seen projectile vomit hit shit from across the room and it's incredibly disgusting. Also depending on how your yard is set up can have some damage also, and this includes your neighbor's yard too. If there are trucks at a teenage party then someone will try to show off and it's a lot more fun for them in someone else's grass. Now I will begin with telling you how to throw these types of parties with really good suggestions. I may not cover some things, but enough is covered to allow for a pretty smooth party depending on how lazy you are.

(House Parties) I will start with the garage and if it is not your main entrance to the house then it will definitely help you plan early. If you do not have a garage then a shed or attic with good storage space will work also. Obviously I am talking about moving all the breakables out of any room that will have people in it. This may take a while, but you will appreciate this since nothing can get broken. Any excess lighting should be removed and this is going to mostly include lamps, or track lighting on a pole. Any glass tables, china sets, and antique furniture should also be moved somewhere. Next is for the rooms that will be occupied. Any room that you would like for people to go in over another room should have the door actually taken off the hinges. Sounds excessive and like a lot of work, but two guys can remove every door in a large house in under ten minutes. Don't be a lazy ass because you will appreciate it later after the party is over. For some reason I have seen that even strong doors can be broken at a party, pretty easily. The reasons that I have recommended this is that anyone who has ever thrown a party before knows that even a good door can be broken at a party, or your frame will be cracked. My best example is when a friend of mine decided to run over a bedroom door like a car hitting a deer because he was a little too drunk. The other reasons include smoking in the room, making out, or unless you don't care. All other doors should be locked with a sign saying that the room is off limits. Halloween parties are the easiest to block rooms because spider web works perfect for getting the point across. If you do not do this then people will assume that any room is open for occupants. Most stuff that would go on would not personally bother me unless it's something I don't care for myself to be done in my house. Another big item that's going to get some attention will be the fridge and your pantry. Try to block off your pantry, but most people will want to put their beer or alcohol in the fridge. Also your friends are going to get hungry so either hide your personal food or just smack the hell out of them for trying to eat it. Many people will go outside or you can even call them the outside crowd because a bunch will never even come in the house. You do not want these people staying in the front yard because I am going to tell you that it is not the best idea for them to be there. Do something to make them want to go in the backyard. For some people this will be cutting the grass at least once a year and the others with a normal yard need to decorate. Put up some tiki torches, sweep the patio or deck, and put some chairs out there. Officers will not see people in the backyard and fewer people will hear the noise from outside depending on where your neighbors are located (Hopefully just beside you). There is not much other stuff that makes a big difference to planning a house party except for ways to make money on it, or getting your kegs on time (don't wait till the last minute). Another small thing will be that if you have musical instruments, put them away. I am mainly talking about drums and guitars. I don't care if you are better than Eddie Van Halen and you are very entertaining. Do not play music at a party because there are always a lot of people that will get tired of it quick. If one person plays, then everyone has to play. A good tip to keeping everyone there is to play a variety of music and include the types that you don't like also, but play it from a cd player. Someone will like it. If you play one type of music all night then you will automatically end up kicking out an entire group of people by doing so (meaning that everyone does not like the same music). Also do not let people put their own music in because from then on, the rest of the night, will be people wanting to put their cd in.

The next parties that you can throw would be on private land, or someone else's land, and they usually work out fine. If they are in the open then it will not last as long, but in the woods along a long dirt road works great. Do not think that just because the road is only a mile long that cars will not get backed up all the way to public roads. I have seen a road twice that long with cars twice that far in less than three hour's time. Who the hell cares about that though? The main objective is to have fun. (Fire) is the greatest thing when it comes to outdoor parties. A fire will not only provide heat and light in the darkness, but will also provide some control on your party. What I am talking about is that your crowd is going to want to be by the fire so that they can see each other and what they are doing. This eliminates a lot of the wandering and sneaking around because there is no reason for it when you have a giant fire. Do not make it too big because it will be seen farther than you think and will eat lots of wood and especially fork lift pallets if you burn those. I have made this mistake before and the fire department came thinking a house was on fire. There is nothing worse than trying to find wood in the dark after about ten beers with nothing more than a lighter to see and your hands to chop. The fire can actually be more dangerous than you will think due to crazy ass boys and girls wanting to jump over it or someone wanting to dump flammables on it. One time we threw a party in the woods and some crazy ass person was trying to light the fire with gasoline. The rest of the story is self explanatory and I still laugh thinking about it today three years later, but I am glad that he was not hurt. The kicker to an outdoor party is that your kegs are going to fit really nicely in the back of a truck. This way when someone calls the police, you can have your kegs moved by the time they reach the front of the line. In the past, this is where my friends and I have screwed up. We waited too long and had to end up dragging them back. Luckily I was just arriving back from dropping someone off and did not have to play rock, paper, scissors for jail time or so they said, but cops have a tendency to play also or try to scare the shit out of kids. Do not be afraid to talk to an officer at an outdoor party because they will respect that much more than a person who stumbles off into the woods. If I am at a party and the cops show up then I will treat it like an adult and handle it like an adult. You will not see me running for my life or trying to hide. I will simply sit on my car until they tell me that I need to leave or until officers leave themselves. I usually answer their questions and a lot of times if they can find out that your not driving and your willing to cooperate then they will just leave you alone (meaning that you do **Not** have to rat anyone out, bad idea, and please take responsibility for your actions. I hate seeing people who do this. I claim responsibility for all alcohol that I consume.) I have done this at about five parties particularly and they simply said carry on and went after the person acting like a dumb ass, running off. These officers drank when they were teens and they obviously know how old everyone is and if they can get some cooperation without chasing people then chances are it will not be bad at all. Everyone parties when they are a teenager and I mean everyone. Hell George Bushes daughters were arrested for it several times which shows that no matter who you are, it doesn't matter. I have seen that these daughters were arrested for drinking, but that does not change what I think about them. I still believe that they are very responsible and they are also great role models. Just because they decided to drink does not make me think that they are bad people like the press has said. Your life will last as long as it takes the earth to blink so don't screw it up by not having fun. Now back on to subject, I would like to tell a story of a particular party that I had a small role in. One last thing and it involves music. At an outdoor party means that someone is going to play music out of their car. Don't worry about the volume, but remember that heavy bass pushed with enough power can be heard from over a mile, but the mids and highs will not rattle their way so far unless amplified.

A lot of people near me that I attend school with like to party near the Arkansas River. It is a setting that makes you feel good. Level land in a nice secluded park, on the river and not to mention next to one of the heaviest police patrolled streets in Arkansas (Real smart, huh). Trust me and it sounds dumb, but for some reason I only see it get busted rarely and I really don't think the cops seem to care much although there has been a few accidents there (a stabbing or two and someone fell out of a truck and cracked their head open, and there's more, but that's all I have seen). Anyways I was a sophomore in high school and I delivered a keg down to a friend who had ordered one. Quite a few people showed up and one went down to the river to talk to the people on the tugboat. The tugboat sits in this certain spot because it is between the areas where barges are known to get stuck. The men on the boat were obviously not to busy and gave a bunch of people a ride over to a sandbar where the party continued. We set up a lot of tiki torches and had a great time. What could be better than a keg party on a sandbar during a clear warm night with tiki torches? There is no limit to the types of places to throw a party. The one thing that I will tell you though is to not leave trash on the ground. Sounds kind of stupid to a lot of people, but if there is no evidence of parties then you will continue to have access to throwing them. Since most people like to just throw their trash on the ground then it will end up hurting you in the long run. I am talking about landowners getting pissed and calling the police themselves and then you are in deep shit because they can press charges, or setting up giant fences and digging deep holes, which makes you have to find another spot. Although I have never thrown a party on private land that I did not get permission for in some way. A good type of advice for this would be to talk to the landowner and offer them some money to do this and maybe cleaning up trash the next day. If you can persuade them then it will not be a big deal to offer them a hundred bucks a party. If you have permission then it will not be hard to go crazy with the population and to make four hundred dollars profit in one night if you can hang onto your cups and not give them out for free, since you have expenses to cover.

Different Types of parties
teenagers experience

This is my favorite part to talk about and the reader probably knows just as much on this section or even more than I do. This section refers to different types of parties that I have experienced and that hopefully you will experience also. Some are good parties that is a lot of fun to be at and some suck really badly and you will find that the only reason you're there is because there is nothing else to do. There are all kinds of parties and this usually depends on the school you go to. Even a school way out in the country can still throw good parties. Some parties that are really good do not even involve the people all going to the same school. Also, I have been to many great parties not involving alcohol directly. You can have parties based on frats, sororities, athletic celebration, celebrating a holiday, birthday, wedding, or just a random occasion and I have details on each. Do not get pissed if something is not covered and if I miss something then email me and I will save it and include with your writing being credited in my next item that I work on. I will try to cover all parties that you will see with some personal suggestions that I hope you will like.

The first one that I would like to talk about is the fraternity parties. I have not been to as many frat parties as a lot of people who will read this or the amount of other types of parties that I have been to. When you go to these parties then hopefully you have been invited by someone that is a member. Do not go to these parties on your own because frat parties are invites only (Most of the time). Some require invitation, some require that you know many of the people, or that you bring two girls for every guy that is there, and the others may include a cover charge (money, dumbass). They are very picky about who is there and if you are not a member then learn to respect it because it's their way or the highway. That's how I would organize my party in that situation also. These parties so far have been the best ones that I have experienced. They are not the most crowded parties, nor are they guaranteed to fit how you like to party and the parties usually follow on the same dates throughout different years. The only ones I have been to are from being friends with a member who allowed me to be his guest or through people I work with taking me to them when I worked at a bar and restaurant. I usually do not know too many people at these parties, but I always meet cool people and have a good time. The alcohol is always free depending on what it is and the house is already set up for parties unlike the rest of the party types. The houses are usually set up with large furniture to accommodate as many people as possible, carpet is generally a bad idea in these places, and there is some type of other entertainment. This can be pool tables, dance floors, permanent bar set ups and a bathroom that will accommodate a few people at once. Bed rooms are usually off limits, locked, or out of the way and there are not a lot of breakable items in the house. This type of set up allows for more parties to be thrown with less cleanup or stuff to be replaced the next day. Most frat houses have more than enough parking to supply the cars, but is not needed seeing as how you cannot just walk off the street to them in less you sneak in or something. People who live in a frat have the connections needed in college along with the reputation of being in the club. Some people hate frats and the people that are in them. These types of people may have not had a chance to experience one of these parties or do not share the same lifestyles as the frat offers. A frat is not something that I would not personally try to be in, but if it were offered to me then I would look into it because I like the parties. They are known for the punch they make and for the kegs that are often ordered. Cops leave them alone and very rarely do they get busted since most of the people are 21 anyways. A lot of people will say that the reasons for not liking fraternities are that it is a bunch or rich stuck up losers. I am not saying this, but there are usually rich kids involved with them, but to me is what makes them so much better because they always make the parties better by being rich. Most of the music that I have heard at these parties is rap or dance music since the beat is sufficient for dancing. Every time I have also seen people throw up and this goes without question at frat parties. There is never a sober person present and most frat boys will drink me under the table when I race them and I can hold a large amount myself, but these guys are off the charts. This is saying that if you are in a frat, then you will actually learn to stuff yourself with alcohol and they will probably kick you out for not being able to drink. The buildings smell of it even when there is no alcohol and there are few fights that take place because that will permanently cancel your invite from what I have seen in the past. Unless you happen to go to the party that is a bunch of red necks who are in a red neck frat which is my favorite. Especially when it is a bunch of good ol' boys that throws them. Do not invite yourself into these parties or try to bribe people because you will save the embarrassment by just waiting till you get invited. If you're in college and your campus has frats and sororities then you will be invited to one if you make friends with people at some point, unless you really suck. Although even if I never go to another one I will still not be heartbroken cause there are plenty of parties out there and if I had to put forth an effort then I don't really care about being at the party unless I help throw it of course.

The next type of party is high school. Just because the party is being thrown by a high school does not always mean bad things and they are very often great parties. There is always a ton of people present and many of these people graduated already so if you are a little older then don't feel out of place. It does not mean that you are the old person there because usually people have some friends that are underclassmen and if you went to the same school then you will probably be alright. These parties do not last a whole lot longer than midnight because most high school students have to be home around midnight. If a fight is going to happen at a party then it will be a party with a larger number of people with no one to regulate it. All the ones that my friends and I have thrown in the past were regulated with fights still happening but like maybe once out of every five parties. These parties are known by happening in a different place every single time (usually). A lot of times there is no set party spot for high school parties, and sometimes there are, but this usually happens for schools that party more than others. The places that they are usually thrown include cleared land, large parking lots, houses where parents are out of town and my favorite which is sand dunes in the middle of a large river like the Arkansas river that requires a boat to get to (I have only been able to experience this once thanks to a large tug boat donating some free services). These parties are either BYOB (Bring Your Own Beer) or they are a full blown kegger with a standard 160 beer keg. If it is even remotely good then there will be a minimum of two 15 gallon kegs which is enough to support quite a few people for five hours which is usually a normal high school kegger if all goes well. A high school party is easy to distinguish from any other because every one there is obviously trying to get close to another person. Usually if a cop shows up then everyone freaks out for no reason unlike other parties where it is handled and everyone keeps partying. The reason for this is that the person who usually throws a party has only thrown maybe one or two. There are plenty of exceptions to that because some throw parties all the time. But when a person is throwing a party at their house while their parents are out of town then he or she might not have thrown a party before. If this is the case then they are unaware of how you should handle cops when they show up. If the cops know that the party is a high school party then they automatically will try to walk all over everyone in the house. If you decide to throw a high school party then read up on the rights you have to defend yourself against cops in any situation because you have more rights against them than you think. They are using their rights so use yours. If you allow a few people over, then unless you stop people that are not allowed over there, then you will have quite a few people on your hands and I am talking up to two hundred people and maybe more, so be prepared. Your party can gain people faster than you can count and very quickly so be careful.

Holiday parties are really cool because you get to set up more of a visual setting. I enjoy them more because everyone is always in a great mood for these parties. I especially enjoy throwing them during Halloween and New Years Eve, but I am only taking small credit on this part since I only do some of the work. My friends have been great when it comes to this and they deserve more credit than me for these parties because it is usually their ideas and they put in more money and I just help fund them and set up for them. We do not usually make all of our money back and I still have lost a few hundred dollars from paying for kegs and decorations, but it does not bother me unless I didn't have a good time. If you fund kegs for your party then do not expect to make your money back, if any, depending on if you charge or not. I have made profit before but it was not what I was trying to do. If you do happen to have money maid on top of what you put down then you did great. I will tell you that some girls will put up a fight if you decide to charge them. The standard price around my part of the U.S. is five bucks for all you can drink. Sometimes girls drink free and if this is the case then do the smart thing and get them different colored cups. A lot of times the beer is free or five bucks which is a great price for all you can drink. Most people do not charge per beer, but I have considered this before when I noticed that a lot of people would drink only two beers and want some money back. The problem with doing this would be that you would lose one dollar bills very fast and would not be able to supply change. My best advice if you need to make your money back due to being low on money is to charge girls. They will bitch about this and whoever hands out the cups will have to listen to it all night long. The one thing that these girls need to know is that they don't get free drinks like that anywhere else and it should not be your fault for making them pay. There will be times when girls get free drinks because they do happen to be girls, but it will not happen all the time. The last note on that should also be to supply some type of punch because quite a few girls do not like beer. Back on to holiday parties is that more people come out to party and celebrate these parties, but then a lot of people will want to spend time with their relatives and use this to be close to their family. Do not go overboard with decorations for your party unless you don't mind losing money or if you feel you will make it back or get to use them over and over. Holiday parties get out quick that you are throwing them and especially if it is a good holiday. There will be many people there that you have never seen before and your crowd will be mixed with all kinds of people. I am talking races, sexes, different schools, ages, and you will have jocks, musicians, comedians or just one giant ass mixture of people. Hopefully there will be no fights or cops because they kind of expect parties on holidays and are a little more lenient, except for the driving part. Holiday parties are the "aw best" and I strongly support the idea of them.

I have only been a part of a few birthday, and wedding parties so it may sound like I don't know what the hell I am talking about cause I probably don't. To start off with, you will most likely end up with a guest list or it will be a private party with a large number of people being invited. If you see people that are there that you know were not invited then it will be best to kick them out before there is too many people and then you would really feel guilty for the more people you would have to kick out. At these parties you will want to see more people that you know than a full blown get drunken party. The best reason to these parties being "invite only" is going to be that you will probably have champagne at a new year's party and some type of nasty looking, but great tasting punch at Halloween. Supplying enough for a larger group would be a little expensive when it comes to funding the party ahead of time. People should dress up for both of these parties and maybe offer some sort of prize (case of beer works great) for best costume on the Halloween party.

Parties are highlights of school because that is when special things happen. Use parties for a reason to stay in school. By staying in school you will know when and where they are so you can use that as an advantage to not dropping out. If you drop out then you have made a big mistake if you like to party, unless you still hang out with people in school. Do not fear going to any party unless you have made many enemies. If you do happen to have enemies and feel like fighting then don't do it near the party cause it will just piss many people off. Your partying will be over for the night due to this. Be careful about parties you go to that you don't know anyone there because then you have to be real careful on what you say to people. Especially talking about schools since this is where your rivals could try to kill you and you might not know which school is throwing the party. If you do go to a party and you don't know anyone, except maybe the person you came with then talk to people to get to know them. Don't be the highlight of the party cause you are obviously there on a thin string. My last statement would be to not crash (sleep) at a party and especially not early (don't drive home either, designate someone). There are twelve million things that could happen to you if you decide to sleep at the party, unless you have a room by living there with a lock on the door, but you are still not safe, trust me. My favorite group of stories for this is that I have witnessed people running through doors that are shut on accident, people punching holes in your doors, or something. Because you have to remember that stuff gets broken at parties and it can be anything. Lamps, walls, chairs, cars, and even trees can be broken because I have seen all these items broken at a party. I have been to parties where someone has been stabbed more than once or knocked out and all kinds of stuff. These were not teenage parties though and the one I am talking about particularly was a party thrown by an adult. No matter how safe you feel at a party and by no means are you guaranteed not to be hurt. The ketch to this is that you are just as likely to see a fight in a bar as you will see at a party, so feel free to have a good time even if you are around a bunch of rowdy people. Do not freak out because something happens and even if it does would not mean that you should necessarily leave. The chances of being picked at random for something bad unless your right next to the person being targeted is not that likely. Parties are weird because no matter how much planning is put into it will still end up with an unpredictable result. Remember that the grounds for meeting new people and building a good reputation depend on how you act at the party.

People at these parties

The main portion of a party or at least the most important part will be the people that show up. There are all types of people at parties and especially with an open party. The types of people that I am talking about are going to be jocks, stoners, rich kids, hippies, frat boys, goody goodies, nerds, delinquents, alcoholics, cheerleaders, hatchas, older already graduated people, losers, and the musicians. I hate this part of the book the most because whether I like it or not means that I have to show good and bad qualities for every single type of person. The flaw to talking about different types of groups is that you will notice how these traits stick out the next time you are at a good party (I am assuming that you only go to good parties).

Jocks usually are the center of attention at certain parties. They have a reputation of being a dumb ass. I believe that is bullshit and they are smarter than the credit awards them. Some are quiet and just want to talk to a few people at a time. Some believe that they are the MVP and deserve everyone's attention at all times although different from the movies. They can hold their own and usually start stuff if something happens. A jock is trigger happy a lot of times and especially when there is no one present to regulate the party, and then it will get out of hand with these people (sometimes). Some are quiet; usually the smarter ones and I tend to see the quieter ones settling down with someone at a party. The loud obnoxious jock that drinks too much in the first thirty minutes of a party tries to get with way to many girls than he could physically handle (unless he has super sexual abilities). Athletes are very unpredictable and I think it is due to many hits to the head depending on the sport. There is nothing wrong with a bunch of athletes at a party unless they act like drunken 2 year old ogres. Other than that would explain the main ways that jocks act like at parties. I am usually entertained by jocks because they are funny when drunk. Many tell great stories that are pretty funny. Overall, jocks are not people that should be worried about too much at parties.

Stoners at parties are kind of a trip to the whole scene. Most stoners are going to be a little quiet at parties. It is not like you see on TV. Which is kind of ridiculous on how a stoner is portrayed on television? You will not see a stoner getting taken advantage of (assuming a female stoner), going crazy, throwing up, fighting, or any of the other loads of bullshit that supposedly characterizes a stoner. If the person is respectable about their smoking choices then they usually go in the backyard or to another room that the owner says is o.k. The reason is that some people just do not want to be around the smoke. I don't like being around cigarette smoke or people shooting heroine (just kidding, never around it). My point is that most people who are stoners at a party are more respectable than the other guests. They don't leave trash everywhere, get into fights, and break stuff (generally speaking). Sometimes you will see someone being an asshole about it and lighting up in the middle of the most crowded part. These people would have been twice as bad if they had chosen alcohol that night. Stoners may not have the hottest girl's attention at a party, but will end up being the ones not going to jail if the cops come (supposing they don't come in). Can't give a weed breathalyzer. I am not trying to convince anyone of becoming a stoner, but I am just analyzing the ones that you will probably see that are stoners at parties. I am not a stoner, but I do know quite a few.

Musicians and parties. Musicians at parties will always try to get girls through something about music. I have been playing guitar for ten years with steady lessons involved for over five years. I consider myself to be a musician although I would not play at a normal party. The reason is that I don't think that people come to a party to see one guy show off for them. Usually a musician will bring some type of instrument to a party or play one that is already there. In turn making other people listen to it and then when they get done is when others want to play. I strongly recommend a person not playing a musical instrument at a party. When people go to a party is where they want to hear a variety of music with each being a complete band and not one drunk guy rambling on. A musician can screw the whole night up and end up making a lot of people leave. Although, I do like talking with other musicians since each and every musician is unique. For any musician reading (don't go to a party to play, you will look like a lame ass even if you taught Jimmy Hendrix yourself)(nobody cares how good you are because there are other places to show this off if you are dieing to). Back on subject> Musicians are fun to talk to at parties because you will always learn something from them. Some are full of themselves and steadily brag, but some are fun to talk to if they can talk about normal subjects. Music is an addictive subject to talk about and when you get set on it, you cannot stop talking about it. A musician is always trying to learn new strategies, techniques, styles, and forms of their music. They will relate this stuff to what the people around them are talking about. It's very interesting because a musician tries real hard to be what they have been classified as. I believe that if your stereo is always a big part of a party then the people who play music will probably have interesting and relevant stuff to say.

Hippies and their bullshit. Everyone knows what a hippie is and everyone has a different definition of how they believe that one should be portrayed. Some people think that a hippie should be a flower child or whatever and that certain clothes, food, and music should stand out with these people. Others believe that they are strictly about drugs, music, peace, or love (I Know that is out of order). I see so many types of people that try to represent a hippy in so many different ways. I also do not believe that any exists today, but if you want to call yourself a hippy then that's fine with me. Usually the ones that I see are a mixture of stoners and musicians squished together. I do not mind hippy type music or even certain hippy type rituals (coded for drugs, biatch). A hippy is a great person to have at a party. They usually do not fight, most don't drink, and all have a unique way of how they look. I am telling you for the last god damn time that I am not describing hippies in general and I am only talking about certain, so called, types that I have seen. Do not email me with your bullshit about how I am wrong about what a hippy is because I am not defining what they are and I don't care either. Dreadlocks are very disgusting, but I will admit that the finished product looks cool. Hippies tend to have girls with them because they have a unique look to them and usually know what they are all about (I am talking about the actual person knowing what they are about). I do not know exactly what a hippie is classified as, but I have covered enough to give a general description.

Rich kids are usually dumb. They are usually very popular at parties because they happen to be rich. Money means everything in life today and you can indeed buy happiness with it. If you can't, then you have forgotten that you are rich. Girls drool over rich kids because their childhood is great. These kids go crazy at parties and are by far the rowdiest ones present. The problem with a child that has grown up with money is that they believe that it will always be there for them and slack off in school by never missing a party. A lot of kids who grow up with money do in fact slack off in school unless they are threatened by something financially (Sometimes does not affect grades though). In other words, these kids think that no matter what happens at the party, their parents can get them out of it. Rich kids scream, drink too much, drink and drive, break shit, and my favorite which is throw the best parties. Their parents leave town often because they have money, leave their kids with plenty of money to pay for kegs, and all kinds of crazy shit. These kids do not even go through much planning on a party and move usually nothing of value out of the way. The thing that I think these people should do better is to watch their valuables, furniture, and anything else that is not theirs. Parents come home to a wreck of a house, probably citations given to their child, but there did happen to be a kickass party on the weekend. Obviously, these kids do not care for what they have been given, or what happens to them as people. I do not mind hanging out or talking to a rich kid because a lot of them are not like that. Maybe they became rich later on in life and did not grow up at younger ages this way (preventing being spoiled). The reason is not important, but how they act in high school and college is. I have never been incredibly rich or incredibly poor, but I do know how it's like to have good amounts of money and to not.

Frat boys need to be analyzed because they are highlights of college life and differ so much at the same time. These guys know that they are popular, can have hot girls, they are guaranteed great parties, and act completely different from one another. Some of these guys will act insane, move around the party at fast pace, and meet every single person that is there in five minutes. Some pass out before the party starts, and some are normal people. The ones that act normal probably do not get as many girls, but they will be more important to the frat in staying off double secret probation though. The crazy ones are fun to watch; they have adapted to the lifestyle of "The Party" and don't give a shit about anything that goes on. I do not care about the difference between either type when I attend these parties. This doesn't happen as often as other types of parties, but is pretty unique. If you throw a party on a weekend and fraternities have lost their normal crowd to your party means that your party is kickass. A frat boy would party on an active volcano if others would go with him. They do not care what happens to them or what goes down at the party. These guys know that someone has their back and they just want to have fun. They obviously drink most people under the table and stand alone with defining binge drinking. These people throw the best parties and some can handle police in a mature way, but others tend to say stupid things to cops.

I have defined the basic types of people that I have seen at parties. I left a few types of people out and did this for a reason. The people that were left out would be computer nerds, and people that were sheltered. It is not their fault that they discovered other humans at the age of 17 and I feel that I should not be responsible for explaining why these people are the way that they are. If this type of person is seen at a party then they will either be incredibly shy, doesn't talk to many people and leaves early. Or they get to a party and discover alcohol, drinks too much, and makes a complete fool of themselves in the process. No one is going to talk to these people and I really don't blame them because their parents sheltered them and they leave the party and put everyone else on the road in danger. When these people go to a party for the first time and they see alcohol, then this is where peer pressure comes in. It might be from another person or they pressure themselves through curiosity to try it. That is normally blamed on other teenagers, or (asshole media), but I blame it on the parents for making alcohol seem like a big deal. If they didn't, then the kid would not be so extremely eager to try it. They would simply know ahead of time that they would need a designated driver and when to cut themselves off.

The other group of people that I did not describe would be girls. I really do not want to be the person who does this because I could write two hundred pages off the top of my head. Girls want to be seen at parties by guys and they do different things to achieve this (unless hatchalike lesbians). Some girls do not drink and this allows them to put their heaviest game on the guy they are after. Some girls drink a little, last longer at the party and are able to leave without someone talking bad about them. The other girls drink way to god damn much and either throw up everywhere, pass out, or get snagged by the first guy that notices how intoxicated they are. Some girls get into fights, while others find one guy and lock themselves in the bathroom all night.

When you go to a party then you will find that the only thing that you have really been observing all night is the people. This is quite obvious, but is the most important to having lots of fun in the long run. You will find yourself wanting to talk to some people and also wanting to stay the hell away from certain people (This is my reason at a lot of High School Parties). Sometimes you will have a choice between a girl playing hard to get and another playing hard to get away from. The only information that I have to give to someone at a party is to not act in certain ways. Do not get really loud, act to drunk, or show off in any way. Who the hell am I to tell someone how to act at a party? I am not telling you how to act at a party. I am telling you ways that will allow you to fit in with everyone. Obviously, you can go to a party and no matter how you act will allow you to sit in with some group, but then others will not want to be around you. I am not ever the most popular person at a party, but I can always go to anyone and start a conversation without them being pissed unless it's Elbert (who I probably did something to piss him off). I am not bragging about this, but if you feel like you can fit in with anyone at the party, then I think that's all you should try to accomplish at the party. Then the rest fits in with having fun and either getting lucky, or feeling like you made a lot of new friends.

Uninvited Guests at Parties

Anybody who has ever been alone for the weekend and invited someone over knows that a few more people can be invited from the invited. Or you could just have a party planned out ahead of time. There are a few guests that will usually show up and they are not quite invited by you or the people you know. These people are cops. If it is a high school party then my guess is that everyone will freak out, run and hide, or start crying. If it is a college party then I'm almost positive that the person throwing it will already know how to handle this problem. For all of you stupid people in high school that decide to do something stupid like run away, hide, or pretend like you don't know what's going on then please smack yourself in the face. This is your house and there is no reason to stop the party for the guests or to make the guests handle your problem. When a police officer shows up to your house then you should automatically go outside and greet them and throughout the whole time stay calm and respectful. Do not go running out saying you can't enter, you can't enter (You will sound stupid and just piss them off when all they want is some answers or cooperation). Ask them what the problem is and ask the officer how I can help you. They will then tell you what they have been called there for and my guess is that it is either too many cars or a noise complaint. They will not write you a ticket for these things on the first offense and it is usually the third one that bites you in the ass. Three strikes your out, right. After the officer has told you what he has come for then tell the officer how you will have it fixed and in a quick way. If he does happen to ask you about why he or she smells alcohol then tell him you will not be allowed to answer this question, they should not be allowed to do too much since you were brought out of the house from their presence to your property. Do not let them into your house and do not allow your friends to come out while you are talking because they will screw up what you are probably handling o.k. If the cop shows up and immediately wants to enter the house then tell the officer that you are going to have to go over a lot before you can allow anything and then begin asking the previous questions. If you happen to have kids drinking in the front yard and the cop happens to see them then you are screwed. The cop will start off by asking for their Identification and if they have any common sense then they will say it's not on them or take responsibility to clear everyone else in the house. Then when the cop comes to talk to you and says that he is going to link you to this underage drinking then you simply deny all of these allegations and ask that those people be removed from your property. They should not have been there in the first place. The last thing you want to do is to avoid them completely because they will enter your house and they will write up anything that they happen to see and the people they see doing stuff if you refuse to go out and handle it. When it comes to a party then I would actually fear a fire marshal more than I would a police officer because they can enter the home due to the safety of the people inside. If they decide to take an officer in with them then they are not going to be so blind inside and you will definitely end up with some sort of expensive ticket from this. As you talk to them, please remain calm and you may find the first time of doing this that your voice is a little scratchy and that you are quite nervous. Remember that the most important thing is to sound confident because it will help and they will think that you know more about what you are talking about. Sometimes sending a sober person out that is over the age of 18 to talk for you helps a lot. They can go out and tell the officer that you are busy with something and that you cannot come to the door. The person can then begin saying that you have given them the full responsibility of handling the problem so that you can remain having fun with your friends. This should be of good reason to have the problem fixed. Usually the officer will come to you and walk onto your property. Do not make them stand at the street because that usually tends to piss them off. Let them come up to the house to speak to you. If you have any brains then you will have the door and blinds shut. You will also have told people to not go outside for a few minutes. Leave the music on and do not turn it up so loud that you cannot hear the officer talking. If you turn everything off then it may seem like you are hiding stuff. If the music has to be turned down a little for the rest of the night, then agree to it. Your neighbors deserve your respect also.

There are two ways that the officer will approach you and I save this for last because it usually lets you know the outcome pretty quick. The officer will simply approach you in a very pissed off mood or in a very concerned mood. They are all doing their job so even if they seem pretty cool then you still don't say something stupid. Say things to a cop in the way that you would to someone like a Mr. Badass type cop that you see in a movie. Remember they do carry very painful objects called guns. If they approach you in a very evil, mean type mood then tell them that you will only talk to them and cooperate if they treat you in a calm way. Tell the officer something like you have very close friends over and you do not want the cop making them think that something is wrong when they party is fine and that you request the officer treat you this way. Some will try to walk all over you and this happens more than any other approach because they are trained to be assholes. I have nothing against this on a normal day when it means something to them doing their job. When the officer comes to the party is when he expects to be the only one that will request something to be done. Many lawyers recommend stopping this behavior and recommend you use it very respectfully and carefully. The lawyers say these things so that you do not pile some stupid case on them that should not ever have made it this far especially when there is no money to be awarded from the state for this. Which, wastes their time and is an awkward thing to hear from a lawyer. I am not saying this stuff to walk over cops because I have nothing against them. In fact, I tend to have more things that I like about them over what I don't like. But, they should treat you with respect also. The other type of approach that you will see is the officer who shows up wanting to show off or not be hated by a hundred teenagers. They may start off saying that you are not in trouble but, they do need you to relocate cars or tone the music down so the neighbors can sleep. Even if the officer seems like the coolest guy you have ever met, that does not mean that you should give him any more heads up than one that has hit you with a nightstick in the face. This is the hardest section to write about because the law for this stuff is different in other states. I encourage you to read more on this subject matter because you will regret not doing it. If you think that you can just throw a party at a house even if it is way out in the woods with the next house being a quarter mile away then you still have chances. I have had friends in different houses that have done this and both parties had cops showing up. One I hear had officers walk all over them from stupidity and the other lasted all night after a hundred cars were moved. Even if only about twenty people are invited you can still end up with hundreds in a few hours. My favorite cop story is when there was a keg party at a local party spot in the middle of the woods. The cops showed up hours into the party and we had absolutely no say-so on anything taking place because it was not our land. The cops that showed up were a bunch of good ole boys that came to end the party in their own way. They started by walking to the center of the party (fire and kegs) and then everyone around this area pretty much became the people throwing it cause we were destined to save the beer. Later on that night is when we found our friends playing rock paper scissors for rides to jail or even the best part which was the emptying of the kegs. Every time the officers would turn their backs is when the real drinking would take place for some. Sounds more like a game of "drink before they look at us" although I did not get to play this game. My point is that the officers will do anything to try to get answers or to the bottom of everything.

They will try to scare you, threaten you, or do other things, but all they want to do is find answers even further. Where did it come from and who bought it? These answers should not be answered because if you accept these questions, then you are not taking responsibility for your actions. If I accept beer then I will take full responsibility for it and that's the end of it. The reason is that if I get a dui, then I am responsible for that and will not try to blame anyone else. I have even had an officer accuse me and my friends of shooting the neighbors house with a paintball gun. I do admit that this would be kind of funny, but we didn't even have a paintball gun (I think someone leaving the party did this). The point is that unless you go talk to the officer and straighten it out then they will not take you seriously and you could be avoiding them for something that they will just drop quickly and leave you alone because you have been falsely accused. Being a police officer is a job just like any and they will still get paid even if they do not arrest you. Most of the time you will be o.k. without cops showing up depending on the location and the rest of the time they will stake out to watch people leave which isn't that bad. Then you get to tell all the little sophomores and juniors that they will just have to party past midnight, but they will think it's the end of the world. The last thing that I will add before I tell what I think of cops personally is that you should not offer them bribes, beer, or something because then you have just dug the hole deeper unless you got a lot of money and then no cop will turn you down. Because if I was a cop then I know I wouldn't. Hell they would probably act as security for your party if you have enough money to offer. But keep in mind they are not your average day super troopers.

I think of cops as a sort of bully in a way that's backed by the government. I do not hate them and I certainly do not usually say bad things about them. We do need them in our society, but I just wish that certain harmless things could be avoided as problems. It would be a lot easier if the neighbors would just simply call over or knock on the door about something that they have a problem with. Well we all know that will not happen when there is a bunch of crazy drunk teenagers next door who can be unpredictable sometimes. Police officers should not be hated for what they decide to do because it is not like in the 70's where fewer things are recorded. The phone calls, cameras in cars, sometimes listening devices are all things that people can use against them if they do not do their job. When you escape the fact that you have not gotten into trouble then you are simply lucky for this. There may be a time when you are really pissed at an officer for giving you a 50 dollar ticket for having your car turned the wrong way outside your house. Maybe you have received a big expensive ticket for speeding two miles over the speed limit on your skateboard. My point is that hating the cops will do you more harm than good. Learn to work with them on stuff and you will appreciate their services a little more. For all of you potheads out there who want to kill cops then that is a different problem. They have to arrest you for these things whether you like it or not or whether they like it or not, given they follow the rules. They have no training to work with you on this and once in a yellow velvet covered moon is when you might escape that. I am telling you now that the police will not even be the biggest worry of your party. Your guests will be the biggest by far and I am talking about demolishing your house, acting stupid, and being the reason for cops showing up. The officer does not want to ruin your life and the biggest flaw to this is that people fear them. Go talk to the officer, it may be something innocent. Even the most respected people in society have to talk to officers at some point. It does not make you a criminal to throw a party if you are willing to handle it.

Questions I face when debating underage drinking

This section will allow me to answer a few questions about underage drinking that I have come across and delivered an answer to. My answer is just as good as the one opposing my own. I like to tackle issues involving this subject head on. Hopefully, I will provide an answer that was questioning someone on how there could be a brighter side to it. There is too much debating on how underage drinking should be handled and I believe I am also right about the certain issues that are explained.

A recent web site that I have read suggests that alcohol related car crashes are around 41 percent of the total crashes. They do not mention how many wrecks are from this statement. Many reports say that around two thousand of these wrecks were from teenagers. This would also leave around fifteen thousand belonging to adults who drink and drive. When someone speaks of alcohol crashes then they usually leave this number separate from teenage alcohol crashes to allow for an illusion to your mind to make it seem worse than it really is. They say alcohol related crashes are the number one killer of kids in the U.S. Trying to stop alcohol consumption in teenagers is not working. There is no stopping it and they keep taking away the safeties that should be there for kids when drinking. If you can't stop it then work on ways to make it more efficient. That will save more lives. Some campuses even offer public rides to your dorm if you cannot drive and this saves the lives of teenagers. Setting up a system with your local city would guarantee the safety of your children. With public transportation to get them home after drinking and places to monitor it and allow drinking would definitely work better than the government's position on it now. True, the government is saving money by avoiding stuff like this and all they have to do is accept the deaths of teenagers. Would the government rather have teenagers die and save money, or to spend more and save their lives? Obviously the only teenagers that would need this would be the ones that are just starting to drink and that they would soon learn how to drink on their own and be responsible if someone would teach them. What if the laws could become harsher for drinking and driving, more ways to not have to drink and drive and then to check the statistics on how many people die per year.

Many say that teenagers have an immature, but positive view of alcohol. It is also very true that teenagers are targets of advertising from alcohol related companies. The point to me wanting to tackle this issue means that I believe these statements are skewed. Teenagers want to kick back and relax in their spare time. It is true that nearly fifty percent of teenagers drink on a monthly basis. I even believe that this is around 75 percent. The only reason that people take this as a bad thing is that they are made to believe that every teenager in this percentile is irresponsible with drinking. Out of this seventy five percent that I believe drinks, does not mean that the majority are irresponsible. I have been a part of many parties where hundreds of people have been drunk before my eyes. I saw one person throw up and one girl tackle too much. We took her keys from her and made her sleep in a room by herself (we stopped her from being pulled over and being raped. Isn't this the kind of behavior that should be rewarded?). Out of a hundred people that were there I only saw two that got a little bit out of hand. I do not even count the dumb ass that threw up. There was no harm done that night and for every five people that I saw meant they had a designated driver. My statistics come first hand and I am not some guy writing statistics that was not there to record them. My views are first person unlike others stopping this that has a narrative view against teenagers and goes on bullshit surveys. Teenagers are not allowed to sit on the committees to make laws, but have to sit there and listen to an older persons view of how it is wrong with no way to debate them.

Many people say that Teenagers are more likely to be raped during alcohol. This again is the governments fault on not trying to regulate what they cannot stop. If adults were forced to drink in ridiculous places, then they too would have the same stats as a teenager. No one can argue this without doing research in an environment that is the same for both teenagers and adults. But, how do you classify a teenager from an adult? What is the real difference from a person who is 18 and one who is 21? They have more experience to life. This experience usually involves education, working, and maybe paying bills. But, do any of these things involve alcohol or how you would act? When you turn 21 and decide to drink then most people probably learn to barhop (not that there is much to learn). Anyone that I have seen barhopping is usually in a group of people with one choosing to drive sober. This would be the same for 18 year olds if in fact it were legal. They would also go to liquor stores, but would not have to drink in places that would make things complicated for them to get home since they could drink at home. Examples could be parks or houses when the parents are out of town.

This in turn would allow teenagers to be around other adults and teenagers more during the drinking process. This would kill many of the rape type incidents that are happening today. Because once again, I say that drinking cannot be stopped.

Many people say that the average age of boys and girls who first try drinking is eleven and thirteen (boys 11 and girls 13). I do believe that this is a little early and I am not fighting for these ages, but then to think that if someone who is almost ten years younger than me can get a hold of enough alcohol to become intoxicated. This is fairly easy for them, but then to think about how easy it is for someone ten years older than them, but still underage getting a hold of it (sounds pretty easy, huh). I am eight years over a recorded average of when some say boys start drinking, but it is still illegal. I am almost twenty years old. That sounds like a strong number, but to say that I am too young to ingest a liquid with alcohol. Well if purchasing alcohol is to easy to do and if it cannot be stopped, then why not try and do something to legalize it and regulate better. Making identification cards more state of the art does not stop anyone from having alcohol in their possession. What's the point of making identification cards harder to copy if most kids have someone buy for them? I usually purchase my own alcohol, but if I could not, then why would it be so hard for me to ask a friend that's a few months older to buy it. They say that alcohol can cause all kinds of depressed teens and suicides. This is true with any age group, but they never tell numbers in proportions for this stuff. Maybe it happens to a thousand kids out of like hundreds of millions. Is this enough to ruin drinking for every single teenager? When you could legalize it and then the kids would not have to be afraid to say when they would go drink to their parents. You would know when they were drinking and could make plans on how to save your Childs life by just going and picking them up or knowing where they were while drinking. Wouldn't you rather know that they were drinking and to help them to not having to drive, then to worry that they might be doing it behind your back to one day find that they died in a car crash. This is the biggest issue stopping the legalization for upper teenagers from drinking when it could save their lives to not avoid it anymore and supplying them with the same circumstances that adults get when they drink. I use to work at a restaurant that provided transportation for customers. Every time that I saw an adult sitting in that car made me smile knowing that their life could have been saved by being in that van. But, then I would be saddened knowing that for every adult receiving this designated service in that van, that there were twice as many kids out there that chose to drink for the same reasons and was not provided with a ride like that except in a police car or ambulance. I will say once again that there may be some higher injuries with teenagers, but you cannot compare them with an adult drinking without providing them with every situation being the same. By allowing designated drivers to give rides to adults who drink, but not to kids who drink is definitely going to cheat some of the statistics. Adults are babied with alcohol and kids actually have to show more responsibility than an adult when drinking.

Things that are not fair that are used to describe teenage drinking, but not adults drinking. Many people will only refer to drinking as a drug when compared with teenagers, but will say something like it is just alcohol for an adult. Why can't the comparisons sit on level fields? There are too many little things that are thrown in with a teenager drinking that sway opinions. This is not fair when trying to persuade viewpoints on something.

I have read that kids are 50 times more likely to try cocaine that drinks alcohol. Kids are 22 times more likely to try cannabis that drinks alcohol. Review over those last two statements a few times. They say that these kids are more likely to try cocaine than cannabis by more than twice as many times because of alcohol. I hate to say this, but that is the stupidest thing that I have ever heard. These types of things are thrown at the public by organizations. They give one sentence to the public and do not tell what the situations were. Did they do their surveys in South Columbia? How can there be an exact number like this without skewing something. Most kids fear cocaine and I do not appreciate this being thrown in to parents because shit like that is not fair to use because it is not true completely. There is something wrong with this survey, and it is either they did not select random people, held it in a cocaine facility, or gave it to cocaine rehab kids to fill out survey slips.

Many people say that three out of five teenagers have had an alcoholic drink in the past month. They are saying that roughly sixty percent of kids have had a single alcoholic drink in the last month. That's not enough alcohol to do anything to anyone and if that is the rate that they are drinking at to be able to prove on a randomly selected month would not pose any danger at all. So in other words, who the hell cares about that, but because it has a high percentage and the word alcohol in the same sentence makes it sound bad. But, it is actually describing a child who gets a glass of wine with dinner once a month. These organizations try to make normal things sound bad. This is not saying that these kids had their first drink in the last month and will get worse in the future. That is saying that some kids who could have been drinking for over a year, but only drink one drink per month. This fact may be very true on what they say, but is skewed on how it is said to make it seem like it is a bad thing. If that is true though, they say a glass of wine (red) is good for you, but when put that way is deadly (ridiculous). Every point that is made on drinking towards teenagers is converted into a form that makes it seem like a very bad thing and even if it is a good thing to start with.

Some say that over 2,000 kids die in alcohol-related car crashes each year. Yes that is probably true and they make it sound like this statement is absolutely horrifying. Where is the rest of the information and where's the comparison on car crashes to adults? For all we know on that statement is that it could have rated for every country and not just the U.S. Even if it is just the U.S. would not exceed how many adults risk this very same death with drinking. Kids are already getting away with drinking on a thin line and the majority of them do not want to risk what they are getting away with by making it worse through driving. What better way to teach them to being safe about drinking than to teach them safe ways to drink. If you do not teach teenagers safe ways to drink then they will not know, so when they do decide to drink is what actually puts them into danger. Parents put off allowing their drinking for so long and do not allow it at all. Your teenager grows up with no knowledge or being taught while in these situations. You wait until your child is out of sight and then you have absolutely no control over their actions. How can a parent say that they would rather their child learn to drink in college than when they were younger and under their supervision? College has more incidents than any teenage lifestyle can produce before college. Why not teach them about drinking while they are still living at home. A parent is not going to be at a college party to tell their child when to stop or how important it is to not drive at the time of the party.

I do not feel like answering anymore questions on this stuff because of all the lying to parents is making me sick to my stomach (I am not going to lie though because I have nothing to lose in the matter). I have a perfectly good reason to all these questions that have bogus answers when presented by the media. I am so tired of seeing everyone talk about how these problems get worse and do nothing, but talk about how they can be fixed. If I can save one persons life through this book, then I will be the happiest person on the planet. I will say for one of the last times that if you do not tell your child and show them how to be responsible while intoxicated will do them more harm than good. Obviously, there is going to be many that do not believe anything that I say. Since you cannot stop it, so accept it, but offer ways to make them safe about it. Before I go on I would like to repeat that picking your child up at parties after drinking is gong to work better. Many kids tell there their parents that they are going to spend the night at a friend's house. Instead they go to a party. I have never had to do this because these kids end up with no place to sleep. I would rather come home drunk and deal with my parents than to not have a place to sleep (not driving home though).

But many other kids are risking dangers through not having a place to sleep after parties because they are afraid to go home. Instead, putting your child in danger, then allow them to tell you when they will be out drinking instead of them doing it behind your back. Then you can let them know that you are there for them when it is needed. Tell your child that when he or she goes to a party that you will pick them up if needed. If your child says that they have someone to drive for them then that should be efficient because at this point means that there is no lies that have to be told. Also if your child needs you for something or an answer on a problem at the party then you can actually help them. The problem with the world today is that people do not want to work with each other, but some just want to make all the decisions. You can not make every life changing decision about your child because whether you want them to do something or not, alcohol is still fun. As long as your child knows that alcohol is fun, then they will offer to work with their parents on it to be able to keep doing it.

How is your child supposed to believe that they should not be aloud to drink when it is legal in the rest of the world for them? How are they supposed to not like it when it is offered to adults in almost any place you can think of? Airplanes, restaurants, casinos, cruises, bars, concerts, games, and wherever, all offer alcohol to adults. Your kid's watch adults consume alcohol which makes them want to do it also. They observe the behavior and act the same way as what they see adults demonstrating a lot of times. I refuse to allow someone to tell me that I am doing something wrong when someone who is only a few months to a year older than me has every right in the world to consume as much as possible. But, I can't even have a single beer.

Some say that many teenagers who drink are depressed or saddened in life? Do they have enough proof to prove that it is because of the alcohol? "Maybe". My opinion on this matter is that most of the kids who are depressed and drink have other issues involved with it (always). The ones that I have seen that drink and were depressed at the same time were because of many personal issues. Most were depressed from losing a girlfriend who they were head over heels about and some were pissed about sports. The drinking helped some to get through it and some needed a little help to get out of the drinking. Alcohol does not depress people (it can make depression worse, but does not cause it). No matter what scientific diagnosis is performed will still have hidden pieces. No matter what scientific result is given on someone, will still have something that is personal that is going to be the true reason for depression. The alcohol can only make it worse, but not create it and sometimes alcohol can actually make depression better. Why should alcohol stand out with depression when there are many other legal things that make depression worse that no one tries to stop? Many pills can make you much more depressed than alcohol because they affect your mood with more strength.

Alcohol is not fair to teenagers. For anyone who knows the true steps to how kids are created into drinkers would know that adults have created it. Your child could be seventeen years old and may not have ever had a drink before. This could be because his parents do not drink or because he tasted something with alcohol that was nasty. He could be watching television and then notices a commercial that was funny and maybe involved nice looking girls in the commercial. Well, what if your child decides to meet with friends that he knows that drink every once and a while on the weekends. They go to a party and he drinks a few beers. This child is probably going to be scared that he may be in a lot of trouble if his parents catch him. This may not be the reason for everyone drinking, but may be exactly the same as a lot of settings for kids who drink for the first time. I do not believe that every teenager gets drunk with their parents for the first time. If a parent would allow themselves to be the ones that teach their kids about drinking and make them feel that they are there for anything that happens, would show that your child would come to you for stuff and not his friends. This is what most parents want and will provide maximum safety to a child drinking. If you finish this book and still want to continue doing things the old way, then fine. If you could be around when your child drinks, then you are there to stop any of these items that your child could be a statistic to.

Other Countries and Teenage Drinking

Does Europe have fewer problems with teenage drinking? Of course my answer is going to be yes. I will review the reasons why with many details. I am also going to speak where they lack behind, so don't object just yet. The statistics are going to show a difference from the U.S. statistics, but with more insight to the true reasons. The reasons that allow Europe to work the way that it does is through experience. By the time that a teenager has hit the age of 18 is a little different than someone in the U.S. That person will be more responsible because they have been drinking already with their parents. I am talking about certain Europeans and not every single one of them. Kids in Europe drink with their families and it is more of a cultural type thing for most of them. It is true that a lot people will say that Europe is more laid back and this helps my argument. If the country is more laid back then it would mean that they are calmer about the whole drinking situation. Teenagers in the U.S. are viewed as being a little crazier and less responsible than the teenagers in Europe. The only reason for this is that people are forced to learn the drinking process on their own in the U.S. and do not fit it with culture. When teenagers come to the U.S. and decide that they like it better here even though it was legal to party in Europe is not because of alcohol or the freedom. These teenagers in Europe prove that when you are allowed to consume alcohol legally, that you learn quickly of how it is not a big deal. Let's say that a teenager is able to buy at a liquor store in the U.S. This person will go to their friends and say something like "This liquor store sold me alcohol" and they will be very enthusiastic about it and think that it's a big thing to them that he or she can now get them alcohol. Well if it were to be legal for this person's age group and he or she went to a liquor store and came back saying the same thing, then his friends would say that I don't give a shit. Then they would carry on with whatever they were doing and not pay any attention to the person. Just because a teenager drinks does not mean that they don't have other stuff to do. If a teenager did not do other things like work, or go to school then they would find out very quickly that they had no place to live or had any money to spend. I do not think that allowing an 18 year old to consume alcohol would make every American become a bum nor would it change the people who do not like alcohol. If you do not like it then having it be legal is not going to make you like it all of a sudden. Some people experience a hangover and never drink again. Some drink to cure a hangover. This is the same with teenagers and adults. Teenagers in this book are adults in every way possible.

Does Europe incorporate culture in drinking? Absolutely, and I don't even know what they are. I have friends that I know that share cultures with their families from Europe. I also happen to know some people from Europe that treat drinking and driving more responsibly than I see Americans. Changing the laws would not affect people right away, but there should be more that goes with drinking as a teenager. Businesses would start up doing stuff for teenagers. Maybe they could have large bars with security and transportation like adults receive. How could a teenager want to drink and drive with something like that being offered? Most people that I noticed in Europe that went to a bar would walk there. Europe is set up in a way that people who live in a city can eliminate the driving by having bars within walking distance. Most of the places that I went to in Europe that I would eat and have a beer were within walking distances from my hotel. If the U.S. could learn how the cultures of Europe can work then maybe allowing this type of thinking to change the U.S. laws would work. If you can provide more efficient ways for teenagers to drink safely then it could be a better agreement. This could eliminate many government funded agencies that try to stop teenage drinking. Which allows spending this money on more efficient ways to allow people to drink safely? If teenagers could drink then they would no longer have to go to ridiculous places to do it. There could be more culture involved with it. Instead of a teenager avoiding his or her parents to drink all the time could allow them to stay home more on Friday and Saturday nights to drink with their parents (only if the person has to drink). Maybe rotating weekends, but not having to drink every weekend. I love to drink, drinking is amazing and fun, but I do not drink that often. Yes, I will admit that I drink maybe once every other week right now. That is less than any adult that I see at a bar. There has been a time when I drank every day in a week and every minute of that day (spring break). Also I went an entire month of not drinking during this past summer (keyword summer when most teenagers drink more). There are times that I feel that I do not want to drink or would rather save my money for other stuff. Many kids feel the same way as I do. Many of my friends are the same way. I have friends that do not drink, I have friends that only drink when someone gives them alcohol, and some that drink way to god damn much. I have friends that are 27 years old and I have never had to ask them to buy me alcohol. I have had minors ask me to buy them alcohol. A minor buying a minor alcohol. I have decided that I will no longer consider buying a minor tobacco because I do not like to be seen buying it. The reason for this is that I no longer smoke and I have quit for a long time now and would like to prevent others. I am not just bitching about age limits in general because I only care about one in particular. Culture is helping my argument. In my family, there is little culture in alcohol. I have lots of Irish in me and lots of Indian. My family's culture involves champagne on New Years, and maybe a little bourbon in eggnog around Christmas. There is also an enjoyment that some of us like to drink a glass of wine while cooking dinner. My mom likes to drink a beer with a little salt in it while she cooks. This is where the culture pretty much stops in my family. What if all the drinking that I do could be put into some type of culture? Drinking margaritas on certain days, or something that runs in a schedule would work fine for creating more culture in drinking. Jesus said that the wine was his blood and this is used for many cultures. Many cultures would have drained him of his blood quickly by being bloodoholics. (I am referring to wine for all stupid people to know). Adults in the U.S. drink to unwind and put smaller amounts of culture into drinking every single day. What's to say that a teenager could not drink in a way that was similar to an adult if culture is going to continue to be put aside? I believe that if alcohol became legal for me (generally speaking since I have already drank at many bars) then I would probably put it into a schedule. I would most likely go to a bar, once a week and switch off on being a designated driver. If this was between two people then I would only drink once every other week. Maybe less, but I would also go to parties and continue to live every last minute of my life the way that I want. Why are we allowing for our one shot at life to be put into someone else's hands on how we live it? Teenagers who have not been taught first hand on how to drink while drinking can experience many problems. This drinking experience faces other problems with many countries. Kids decide to leave the country for spring break and go to places where the government will leave them alone on how they decide to party. For example, I would like to demonstrate that for this spring break I am planning to go somewhere in Mexico. I thought about Cancun, and then I think about how crowded it will be with other Americans. The thing about Mexico is that I can go explore another culture and have more fun than being in the U.S. In Mexico is where I can walk to bars from my hotel. I will be able to walk down the beach barefoot, with my toes in the sand, shirt off, and a nice cold beer in my hand enjoying spring break on a sunny day. I will be with my friends enjoying the nice warm weather. If I decided to do something like this in the U.S. would mean that it would suck a little more. The U.S. is more spaced out on food locations and being stricter on the rules. I would love to go to Gulf Shores, California, or some fairly exotic place for Spring Break in the U.S. I would also have less to enjoy by doing this. I would love to be able to support my country through giving tourist money to my neighbors, but I do that all year through normal taxes and there is nothing extra special to make me want to put vacations like that back into the U.S. Exotic clubs in Mexico are more affordable than the U.S. There are many factors to my statements that I love to explain. If I decided to go to these places in the U.S. for spring break would mean more work on my vacation. I would have to take the entire weeks worth of alcohol with me and in turn loading the car up quite a bit more since I drink like a fish on Spring Break (taking fake id's to coastal cities is not a good idea). This would eliminate me taking a plane and having to drive. I would rather fly to Mexico, Canada, or anywhere than to drive to a place in the U.S. The next reason would be that I could not drink in public during spring break. This means that I would have to drink in the hotel room and walk back and forth from the beach. This is only if I did not want to risk getting into trouble. Other reasons would be that if I decide to go to a club with my friend's would mean that we would have to drink ahead of time and find one in walking distance. This also cancels out the millions of dollars that these states would get during spring break. My friends and I would only contribute a small amount of money through buy-ing drinks at clubs, but when all teenagers start coming back to the U.S. during spring break would really rack up quickly. The last argument that I would make would state that if someone's parent wanted to go to a city with their teenager during spring break would actually not be awkward anymore as far as the drink-ing goes. Today is where no teenager wants to be with their parents during spring break and would like to go as far away as possible. The last spring break that I participated in involved eating, sleeping, playing football, swimming, and drink-ing. If it was not for the drinking part then I would not have cared if one of my parents went, but I would spend most time away from them. Although, since it is spring break I would want the craziest time possible. The last several spring breaks were me and my friends like most teenagers do. Spring break means a lot to me and so does my summer. I still would not want my parents there anyways and they haven't been a part of my spring breaks in the last three years. I work hard for these breaks and I will not choose to be sober all the time to enjoy them. My parents can tell me to not drink and they do. If they try to stop it completely then I will move out. I will come to an agreement with them if they ask, but only if I get to set some terms. My terms would be that I get to pick what I drink, when I drink, and how I drink. I would agree to all other terms that they offer. It may seem like I have left no other terms, but there are some very important ones left. My parents could say that I have to keep up my grades, stay out of trouble, and promise to call them or someone else if I need a ride. These terms are items that they can manage, instead of keeping it a secret. If it were a secret and my grades were to drop because of alcohol, then they would have a problem with finding the problem. This could also be put into culture. The culture of staying smart, positive, and on top of things with kicking back and relaxing being a result of following up on this culture. I would love to research the cultures of my Irish ancestors and Indian ancestors. Maybe bringing them back into my family would be fun and give us more to celebrate. Sitting around a campfire with a piece pipe and talking about stuff would demonstrate my Indian side although I would not do this because it sounds hokey and stupid. The only culture that I have from my Indian side is that many people in my family hunt animals. We own land in two places that even has pieces of arrowheads that we find in the fields to demonstrate our lost culture. My Irish side obviously has drinking involved with it like any Irish person does. There is more Irish in my blood than I know what to do with. My dad even has natural Irish colored hair along with his sister, mother, and his other son. Symbols of Irish culture to me include old pubs, bagpipes, and ale. I would not mind going to Ireland and participating in the Irish dances and culture that they still share. Culture stays with Europe and works for them to controlling their teenage alcohol problem a little more. In Europe, it is not uncommon to go barhopping with family members. Families look out for each other and should be allowed to drink without the older one getting in trouble for supplying the younger ones with alcohol (supposing they are not too young). They will go to bars and celebrate their culture through slamming ales and dancing with many other things involved with their culture. The U.S. is so much different because there are clubs that represent all cultures, but do not do it in the same ways. Culture is very important and I believe that it would help a lot, if it could be regulated with teenagers a little more through drinking.

How does Europe actually view alcohol? Many people view Europe as a place that does not regulate their citizens as well. What I have to say to this is that it is not needed with their citizens. The biggest crime that I am aware of is purse snatching or at least the most frequent. I do not hear of as many murders and violent crimes like that as in the U.S. Many people in Europe are very happy with their government and they may not have as much money as the U.S., but they are happy. Europe has had the time to settle down and they have had more time to learn of how laws should be set. I see Europeans as being stronger in knowing how things should be. Why would the U.S. be so concerned about what teenagers do to their bodies? It is not that extremely harmful to drink every once and a while as a teenager. Alcohol is not that big of a deal and when things have this sense is when people can treat them this way. When I say a big deal is when I am referring to if someone decides to drink, but not being in trouble for it. If it is not a big deal to be able to drink, then many will not treat it like it is a big deal. I see alcohol as a way of being a part of life. I see people happier with each other and even madder with each other, but if they come back then it is stronger. I have two friends that I know and they love each other (I think). It is a couple that I have seen together for a very long time. I have seen alcohol make them extra happy with each other and I have also seen them extra angry with each other. I believe that any time that they argue does not have to do with alcohol, but that they really do have reasons for arguing. Alcohol does not just make people pissed off for no reason. Alcohol may trigger emotions a little stronger than normal, but I have not seen it affect people that bad. Pills are worse for triggering emotions. I hate pills. Many are legal though. Back on to subject (sorry). Anyways I would like to explain more on how Europe views alcohol. Europe's position with alcohol goes beyond the drinking of it. Many special types of recipes are created there and offer amazing taste. Many of the recipes used in Europe are older than the country that I live in. Alcohol is a part of the tourist attraction in many ways. There are many castles that I attended in Europe that had breweries inside the castles. It was part of the tour to offer samples of wine and to sell the people a bottle if they would like. In the U.S is where you would be put in jail for something like this, but it's pretty harmless. Europe is also famous for their beer garden. This garden offers thousands and thousands of different types of beer. This offers a part of every culture that they share with tourists. Recipes that demonstrate times of war, dancing, and many other old events, that took place or resemble these times. Europe has used alcohol to demonstrate many different types of ways for how it is used. The U.S. has pretty much only developed a market on drinking for the sole purpose of getting drunk. If I was offered to get really drunk off of one type of beer that was really good or to try thirty types and not get drunk? I would choose the thirty types over the one good type, supposing that it was maybe two swigs per beer instead of getting drunk off of a larger quantity. I enjoy alcohol more on knowing the different tastes and types that are out there. Many teenagers like to drink a lot and I love to also, but the point is that this is not all the time. Many teenagers could care less about the alcohol and would rather to just drink it. Europe does not share these same traits as we do and they enjoy alcohol in many different ways. The kids in Europe grow up with alcohol being a part of their lifestyle. It does not become new to them when they leave home for the first time. They are used to it and know how to handle it in any situation. Finding a driver, or even managing what you consume is not even a big issue with many Europeans. When a country can change the way that alcohol is consumed, then they have created something special. Many women in the U.S. like to drink a glass of wine with dinner and, like to choose different types to compliment the different dishes that they make. I believe that this culture was invented by a European country. But this one type of daily ritual is enough to satisfy one group of people in the U.S. Maybe if every age group or type could have a certain way of drinking could allow for everyone to be more responsible.

Many people would say that a lot of countries have liberal type drinking laws for teenagers. The way that I view this would be that these countries give the citizens more freedom on the drinking by not caring as much. This can always have some bad effects with certain people, but may not show for the entire population. A lot of kids will have an easier time purchasing alcohol in a way that has an effect that is similar to these laws. It will not have as big of a deal with the way that alcohol is viewed through being able to buy.

Maybe, all teenagers in other countries act differently because they have stuff to lose. The teenagers in Europe, Mexico, Canada, or any other country actually have laws to lose on how they behave. The teenagers in the U.S. may have a less responsible way of acting because they have nothing to lose as far as changing laws. If the teenagers all know that the laws will change to being allowed to drink would quickly alter their decisions. I am saying that teenagers in Europe have to treat drinking responsibly so that it does not become illegal for them. Many do this and a lot share the responsibility for different reasons. Maybe allowing the alcohol for teenagers of certain ages in the U.S. with some exceptions would allow for more responsibility to be accepted by them. Most teenagers know when they look stupid or show poor characteristics with alcohol and the majorities do show safe responsibility.

Europe has been discussing many changes that will take place with the teenagers and adults who decide to drink. They are talking about raising punishments for people who decide to drive in an intoxicated manner. I agree with making the laws for dinking and driving worse because I am concerned with the safety of it. Europe has been discussing ways that they will help people to not having to drink and drive. This is mostly by providing transportation to the citizens who need it. They are researching better car technology, but this does not sway the driving part, but tries to allow people a safer ride while driving drunk. I do not believe that this is a good path, but allowing for more transportation during later hours would be sufficient to supplying people with safety. I think that the U.S. should just give these laws a shot and see how they work. The U.S. has a larger market open to supply more people with alcohol and safer ways to enjoy it. My city has just installed new city transportation that runs on tracks and electricity. It is a trolley car that transports people. I am not supposed to go downtown and barhop and use the trolleys to get from bar to bar because of certain laws. Are there any more reasons that I can think of that should support older teens being able to drink? Yes, but the government creates new reasons every week that are changed into a bad thing from whatever should be converted.

How are teenagers supposed to get tired of alcohol when most cannot drink every night? If a teenager was able to drink every night then they would obviously get tired of it at some point. I am not saying that they should drink every night because this is bad, but if it were allowed then most could care less. This is the reason that many teenagers in Europe decide to not drink every night. When a teenager in the U.S. is only able to drink every once and a while then he or she is going to want to do it every time that it is offered. Unlike when they are allowed to do it when they choose and it would not matter for them to wait till there is a better time for drinking to be done.

The laws on alcohol are so strict in the U.S. that it is very confusing in a global sense. Teenagers that are my age are allowed to drink in most countries, except the U.S. As a teenager in the U.S I am not even allowed to serve someone an alcoholic beverage. Does this type of stuff make any sense? What could possibly happen with someone that is my age serving alcohol? I could take a sip of a drink while carrying it to a table and hope that no one notices. It would be absolutely pointless for me to take a sip of someone's drink because it would have no effect on me at such small amounts and would also be rather disgusting to risk losing a job over a tiny sip. I think I would rather get alcohol on my own than to do something like that. Is there a bigger reason for me not being allowed to serve alcohol? I used to work at a restaurant that served a lot of alcohol. My position was a busser and I also served coffee, water, and many times soft drinks. The bussers were a big portion of keeping the restaurant on top for being a great place to come to. My favorite part of the job was being able to help people instead of just cleaning after them when they leave. I was not able to go to the wine tasting to learn about what was served at the restaurant that I was employed at. Many times I would get asked about what a certain type of beer or wine would fit what they were looking for the best while waiting on their waiter. I could not say because my answer would be wrong. I also know that it would not be my place to describe it to them since I was only a busser. I would like to be able to describe something like this to them since I like to learn about different types. What is so wrong about a teenager being allowed to try different types and explore the different feelings that you get from different types of alcohol. The rest of the world is allowed to drink whatever they want and the U.S. has to sit in on everybody's business for what goes on. I am surprised that the U.S. has not tried to set other countries laws for them since we have to control everyone's lives.

How I Think the Laws Should Be

I agree with everything that the government has created a pretty safe drinking experience for an adult and that they are capable of the same for teenagers. You cannot stop an adult from drinking if they choose. You cannot stop me from drinking if I choose. If I do something that becomes a hazard for me or people around me, then I will gladly listen to someone and stop drinking if they ask. I have never been in a fight while I was drinking, nor have I ever found myself trying to take advantage of someone. I think that the laws should be changed on the ages of who is allowed to drink in the U.S. I am old enough to do anything that has an age requirement except drink. Many of these things allow for more responsibility to be shown than the alcohol does. I believe that the government is wrong on a few things and they will not admit it. I have told of ways that money could be redirected for teenagers to have safer drinking experiences and I have listed ways that the laws would make teenage drinking safer to actual be legal. There are many ways that the laws could be changed so that it would allow for a more efficient way of teaching teenagers to drink responsibly.

The first type of setup that I have come up with will copy one that I noticed in Europe. I do not know if this was the official law, but many restaurants enforce the drinking in a certain way. This setting allows for a teenager to learn drinking in a more responsible manner by allowing them to drink in these ways. As a teenager, I visited Europe with my grandparents. The reason for going to Europe was for a vacation and to not drink for the sole purpose of being intoxicated. Going to Europe for me is probably going to be a once and a lifetime opportunity and I wanted many sober memories so that I never forget them. I visited many museums, famous monuments, and many different countries. The drinking was fun to be able to share, but I would not have minded if it was not there. I was sixteen at the time that I visited Europe. When I would visit restaurants in Europe meant that I was aloud to have beer or wine with my dinner. I could have abused this, although I would not really want to do this for this type of vacation. It was not spring break and since I was with my grandparents, taught me that when you go to a restaurant to eat should mean that the drinking should be put to a minimum (it is not a bar, where I would go to unwind and relax). I cannot say that I was guaranteed to be served alcohol by myself because I did not try it. I believe that this type of regulation works well to allow teenagers to drink responsibly and to learn about drinking. Waiters are taught to not put up with ridiculous behavior and are quick to stop someone from making a fool of them self. Europe allows people to make their own mistakes and in turn allows people to deal with certain things on their own. I do remember that when I went to buy a bottle of wine to bring back for a collectible is where they wanted to make sure that I was a certain age. I believe they asked for me to be at least eighteen years old to purchase closed alcohol. The reason that I believe for them asking this was that I probably looked a little young at the time. So my point to how these rules are set is that they allow teenagers to purchase alcohol if they can either monitor them or know that some-one of a good age is going to monitor the teenager when it is consumed. This means that they are allowed to drink in bars because they are watched. If I would have bought that bottle of wine by myself, then the cashier would not have known what the circumstances would be when it was consumed. She would not have known if I would drink the whole bottle at once or a glass a day. The truth is that the bottle was for my mother and it still has not even been opened. This type of action allows for Europe to contain certain responsibility for teenagers drinking. Another factor would be that I was American. A citizen of this country could probably buy the bottle without any trouble and assuming the cashier knew this. Kids in Europe do not have to hide from their parents while drinking because they can drink with them legally. A parent in Europe is not going to allow their child to drink themselves to death before their eyes. A parent will cut their child off if it is needed and whether or not it is legal. This would demon-strate many ways on how this could be dealt with in the U.S. Allowing teenagers in the U.S. to purchase beer or wine in a restaurant with their parents should not cause too many problems. Even if the teenager is not with their parent should not cause problems in restaurants and bars. This child will have two years of very light drinking before they turn eighteen or hit college. Then allowing an eighteen year old to purchase alcohol at a liquor store is not going to be a big deal. This would also allow for an easier procedure on regulating teenage drinking instead of always trying to find where it is happening and stopping it. Why is everyone afraid to let the U.S. become a more laid back and more cultural type of country? What is wrong with allowing a parent to teach their kid safe drinking methods? I would personally like this better as a parent myself. I want to be the person to show my child how to drink, be responsible, and know when to stop for any situation like driving, or sleeping in safety. I do not want to just have to go on the government telling me that I have to tell my child "no" and hope that they obey this with no sure way to find out unless something bad happens. I would rather my child drink in my house, under my supervision, than to worry thinking that he or she is out in the world drinking irresponsibly without knowing. If my child could tell me when he or she was drinking then I would tell them that I am there to pick them up if needed. The only way that a teenager is going to call their parent for a ride in this situation is to know ahead of time that the punishments are excluded. I would rather my child call me from a party and say that he or she needs a ride, or the reason for why they will be so late getting home. I do not want to drink in front of my child and then have to discipline them for the same thing when I could monitor their drinking. I would not let my child drink at any earlier age than I have myself because I was careful to choose for myself when the time was right. The earliest would be sixteen that I have ever felt the true intoxication from. I know that I could not stop my child from drinking if they really felt passionate about it. I am assuming that it does not happen all the time. If my child's grades were to drop, fights started to happen, or any other bad thing, then I would definitely get them back on track. My point here is to save the life of my child and not risk having them killed. I would much rather know that my child was drinking and that I could just pick them up, or talk with them instead of turning my head and hoping that they get through the night safely. This is my biggest suggestion on how things should be with teenage drinking. This is to allow for the kids to learn responsibility that goes with drinking and to not just say no and hope that they learn the responsibility on there own later in life.

My next suggestion would allow teenagers of certain ages to drink in bars. I am thinking that government issued cards could be given to kids that they can show to allow them to drink. I am also stating that if this child is caught doing something irresponsible with drinking and if some punishment needs to be given than there are punishments for this. The worst punishment would probably be the loss of their card to drink with and being put in jail. I do not debate any drinking and driving laws because I agree with them. I also would not complain if the laws were made stricter and other violations also. Some people may say that the child could pretend like they lost the card when they get in trouble to be able to hang on to it and continue drinking. My suggestion on this one does go a little further than a single card. The card should have an encoded text that cannot be copied and a picture. If the card was put in with some type of electronic library then it could be swiped to know who should be denied. Also if the teenager has been drinking, then the card would have been used for alcohol, so whoever confiscates it would also know that it was somewhere around to be found. This is to allow kids to drink and actually have a lot to lose for being irresponsible. This includes getting into fights, and driving. A teenager will not want to risk the trouble knowing that it could stop them from drinking for a very long time. This system obviously goes with drinking in public and purchasing at liquor stores in public. This is also where the main problem lies with teenagers drinking. If you cannot stop it then work on ways to make it more efficient to see if this can save more lives. Why should this system stop with upper aged teenagers? Why not allow adults to use these cards, also. Then the government could actually start trying to save alcoholics. Adults have problems also, so why not try to fix teenagers and adults with one system. I believe that either one of these systems would work better than trying to stop teenage drinking completely because I am more concerned with how many act instead of looking for dangers to find and use against them.

Conclusion

By now, everyone knows that I am trying to change the age restriction on alcohol or at least voice my opinion. I have already said many times in this book that I do not care about having to be twenty one to consume alcohol. I have also said that I only drink on occasions. I am only concerned with saving the lives. I looked into many ways for improving this without lowering the ages and I did not see anything that would work as well. If someone came to me with a way to stop me from drinking, then I would simply say fine. I will wait the next year or few months depending on the publishing time until I am twenty one. There has been nothing that has done this, though. States can keep making their driver's license more and more complicated. This only stops many teenagers from going to bars where they will be monitored like an adult does and in turn making them safer. Since the states do stuff like this, also means that most alcohol that teenagers purchase comes from a liquor store. If a person has to buy alcohol for the first one hundred times from a liquor store, then it also means that they have been drinking in private. There are many more dangers to teenagers drinking in private, so why not allow them to go to bars where they can be taught on how to treat it more responsibly. The government keeps setting themselves up for the deaths that are caused too and from teenage drinking. The more that they make alcohol more complicated to get and drink, the more dangerous it will make it for the teenagers when they do get it. Teenagers do so much like school, sports, work, and they have many things that they want to celebrate. Why should something like this stand its ground against teenagers? If the laws are changed at some point to similar ones of what I have stated, then what would it change for me. For me, it is not going to change anything, except that I will have to look into designated drivers for when I drink in public. Right now, I only use a designated driver on very rare occasions since I do not drink in public too often. The one thing that I will have to remember is that if I mess up then it could affect many teenagers. Why would I want to mess up things for teenagers in general when all I have to do is act responsible with alcohol? The amount of teenagers that I know drink on this very day is a set number. If alcohol would become legal for the ages that I fight for would not change the amount of teenagers that I know today that drink. The teenagers that I know, that do not drink have chosen not to because they do not like it. The ones that I do know will not be affected either, but we would treat it the same and act the same because I do not act stupid because it is illegal, but to save embarrassment. Hopefully you have not forgotten the good points that I make that will save the teenagers life from what is being stolen. I am only interested in making things safer and it could allow teenagers to drink under certain circumstances. I think about stuff that needs change and the only way to change something like this is to sacrifice the view that America has adapted and take a risk. The risk is worth it if it can save lives. If drinking should become legal for a teenager to put them in the certain situations that are needed to make them safe then why not try it. Why should an adult receive extra help with drinking responsibly and a teenager have these same safeties taken away out of greed for fun? These safeties have been removed from teenagers to build up the statistics needed to persuade parents from disagreeing with it. Teenagers are underestimated with their responsibility and actions.

I have just arrived back from a party that I went to for this part. The time is around three in the morning. I went to this party sober and remained sober. The reason for this is that I wanted to observe people drinking with a stronger state of mind. Normally I do drink at parties and I enjoy them. This particular time I observed the people that were not twenty one and the ones that were twenty one. I noticed one girl who got out of hand that took some pill with her alcohol (probably a bar of xanax). She fell a few times and I had to catch her twice from smashing her face into whatever she would have fallen on. This is an example of being irresponsible with alcohol (she was over twenty one). Another person was close to this situation (He was under twenty one). I have been to parties before that the girl was at and I noticed that she was not anywhere near that condition. My point to this is that she was not allowed to be completely irresponsible. The other teenagers took her home and this is what matters. The drinking is not important because the girl learned her lesson. She will wake up with bruises from falling. I did notice some teenagers leaving the party that did drink alcohol that were driving home. Some carpooled and the drivers would be safe in a twenty one year old's shoes, but not being nineteen and twenty. The driver had a beer and he would be safe if pulled over, but the other driver was only twenty and would go to jail for this one beer. There were people at this party being irresponsible that were over twenty one and under. It was about a fifty/fifty margin though.

How can alcohol be stopped with teenagers? You can enforce stricter laws, higher fines, increase police patrol, hire more security, set up more road blocks and do whatever to stop it. They are all effective on stopping things that have already started or things that are only delayed. There is nothing that can be done to stop underage drinking. Lectures, curfews, or anything cannot stop it. A teenager can just offer someone money for alcohol, use a fake I.D. or whatever the hell they want to buy alcohol. What's to stop it? A teenager can spend ten minutes on the internet and twenty bucks for supplies to make their own alcohol. Hundreds of websites offer free instructions for making alcohol with items that cannot card teenagers for. Who could possibly know that a teenager was going to make beer by having a bucket, a distillation tube, and glass jar sitting in various places in their room?

The problem with alcohol is going to get worse and worse. I have lived with the rules this way for a long time now. Trying to stop the consumption of teenagers and alcohol cannot work. All of this wasted time and money is just supercharging the fire. Spend the money on ways to allow kids safe drinking and learning for their future reference. That is a cause for good. Offer rides, allow them into bars, and set different privileges for different ages. This allows for supervising the ones who need it while learning to deal with the intoxicating effects of alcohol. All I am saying is that new methods should come into existence. If a way for teenagers to not drink alcohol could come up then fine, whatever. I would be bummed out about it, but I would then go on with my life sober. The point is that this is not possible so make it more efficient. If you can't beat them, join them. Allow interactions to happen between adults and teenagers. It is safer for the knowledge of a teenager to have experience with alcohol under supervision several times than by being alone with friends for the first time. I am running out of things to talk about so I am going to end my book now. I hope that I have inspired you to think more positively or convinced you to try new approaches with your child or as a teenager yourself. Most of all I hope I have saved at least one person's life through my suggestions and research.

Love,

Andrew Cornell

0-595-34947-1

CPSIA information can be obtained at www.ICGtesting.com
Printed in the USA
LVOW050257140513

333667LV00001B/58/A

9 780595 349470